VERMILION
~ SEA ~

A
NATURALIST'S
JOURNEY IN
BAJA CALIFORNIA

Books by John Janovy, Jr.

John Janovy, Jr.

VERMILION SEA

A NATURALIST'S JOURNEY IN BAJA CALIFORNIA

HOUGHTON MIFFLIN COMPANY

Boston New York London 1992

For information about permission to reproduce selections from
this book, write to Permissions, Houghton Mifflin Company,
215 Park Avenue South, New York, New York 10003.

Library of Congress Cataloging-in-Publication Data

Janovy, John.
Vermillion Sea : a naturalist's journey in Baja,
California / John Janovy, Jr.
p.   cm.
Includes bibliographical references.
ISBN 0-395-57649-0
1. Natural history—Mexico—Baja California—Popular works.
I. Title.
QH107.J36   1992   91-25101
508.72'2—dc20   CIP

Printed in the United States of America

HAD 10 9 8 7 6 5 4 3 2 1

Contents

Preface

Back in the sixties I met a student named Raphael Payne. Since that meeting our respective careers have prospered in academia, mine at a large university, his at a small one. Then one day he decided to finish his doctoral studies. So Rafe returned to Nebraska on a sabbatical to study worms. Between our earlier and later encounters, he had traveled for several years with students in Baja California and had acquired a sense of reverence for that long finger of desert.

Of course Rafe and I talked about the remarkable book by John Steinbeck and Edward Ricketts, *The Sea of Cortez: A Leisurely Journal of Travel and Research.* The narrative portion of that book, known as "The Log," has a profound effect on every biologist who reads and understands it. At one time it would have been impossible to be a professional scientist and not understand *Sea of Cortez;* its combination of childlike wonder, anticipation, and discovery reflect pre–World War II biology. But in the waning hours of the twentieth century, our great institutions seem almost consumed by their search for solutions to problems of practical, thus economic, significance. The consequent scramble for grants and patents has become an end in itself. Nowadays it's rare to find a scientist who'll tell a dean that one's research is done only to satisfy a personal curiosity.

But biologists who study whole plants and animals, especially those of no agricultural importance, tend to identify with Steinbeck and Ricketts in their *Sea of Cortez* roles. Steinbeck's narrative gives legitimacy to the act of exploration for its own sake, to curiosity devoid of any utility, and to long talks about ideas rather than arguments over money. So, ignoring the fact that Ricketts sold biological materials for a living, we reread the book periodically, in the way that some people return, time after time, to a particular place for spiritual renewal.

During one of my talks with Rafe, I expressed a desire to do two things: see a live, wild, whale and put my hands into the Gulf of California, where Steinbeck and Ricketts had grubbed for starfish. I'd more or less earned my right to such a trip by volunteering a few years earlier to teach a university course entitled Invertebrate Zoology. Now "Invert" is a particularly intimidating subject; at least a thousand different courses can be offered under the title. There is no simple way to describe the information at one's disposal. But even in Nebraska you can't begin to offer Invert without also becoming the proud keeper of a seductive and demanding assemblage: a marine aquarium.

I set up five very large temperature-controlled saltwater tanks in a room in back of the teaching lab and placed them in the care of an extraordinary young woman named Ralene Mitschler. Before the semester was over, she learned to lavish the most sensitive attention on these tanks and their denizens. Under her possessive and never-blinking eye, crabs and snails flourished, mussels stayed alive, barnacles raked through the brine, red anemones spread their knobbed tentacles and, in the highest of compliments nature can give back to a human, the little purple nudibranchs of the genus *Hermissenda* came out of hiding in droves. I tried to memorize genus names. The students, more alert than I to what was going on, put a sign over the door to the aquarium room: Ralene's Ocean. The sign is there to this day.

To fill these tanks with wonder, we ordered animals from Pacific Bio-Marine Laboratories, Inc., a company with a name close enough to that of Ed Ricketts's former Pacific Biological Laboratories, Inc., to inspire a rereading of *The Sea of Cortez.* Plastic foam containers arrived on our loading dock; we tore into the wrappings with razor blades and scalpels, then lifted out the plastic bags, holding them as if they were samples from another planet, imagining what the encrusted rocks and shells would look like under a microscope.

The array of creatures that emerged from this material over the next ten weeks was simply staggering. They were exotic but at the same time hauntingly familiar. Every zoologist knows a great deal about hundreds of kinds of animals, sometimes from the literature, sometimes from having encountered them. But except for those that you specialize on, the superficial familiarity only underscores the ignorance you feel when a tiny scale worm slips into the crevice between a couple of attached clams or when a bit of vegetation suddenly metamorphoses into an angular skeleton shrimp, and you have no idea what to call either one except, respectively, "polychaete" and "caprellid."

Over time the simple question "what is it?" can be answered, not always easily, but nevertheless at progressively lower taxonomic levels. Books are ordered; friends are consulted. One searches for and finds keys, and in so doing one discovers once again the paradox that a device created to help identify unknown specimens is actually of the greatest use to those who are already most familiar with the animals. Thus the more you study polychaete worms, the more valuable you find the literature about them. Nonscientists generally can't fathom this mystery; in their world, if you learn something, you *know* it. In our world, however, when you learn something, that knowledge is mainly an introduction to the puzzles that characterize the specialty.

But of all the questions raised by an encounter with exotic fauna, the most unanswerable one is, Why did I not choose to study this species years ago? The question is a constant reminder that a single life is an evolutionary trajectory constrained at the beginning by boundary conditions and directed throughout by the very accomplishments it strives for. Maybe I did not become an expert on sedentary polychaetes because there were no sedentary polychaetes in Oklahoma when I chose to try to become an expert. Maybe I was not intelligent enough or did not have enough insight to become the world's authority on tube worms. But I'll never know.

When the plastic bags arrived, however, filled with salt water that only a few hours earlier had been in the Pacific Ocean, and the rocks inside were covered with creatures I had never touched alive, then I was suddenly aware of my vast ignorance. And it was in such a mental state that I said, "I'd like to go to the Sea of Cortez" to Rafe Payne.

No sooner were the words uttered than we had a contract. Eventually I did go to Baja California. And I wrote about the trip. The writing was a reflection on a pilgrimage, on the search for something I knew was there in Baja California, the spirit that had turned a great novelist's mind away from the affairs of men and back toward the natural world. No matter how old, how accomplished, how involved in the business of doing the business, biologists need to go to a country where the fauna and flora are wondrous enough to capture our full attention. None of us is good enough, or sophisticated or successful enough, to escape that need.

Rafe Payne teaches at Biola University, a relatively small, church-affiliated school in La Mirada, California. He offers a winter-break field course called "The Ecology of Baja California" to college students from all over the country. Groups from Nebraska Wesleyan regularly participate in the program along with their teacher, Glen Dappen. Glen is a close friend of mine, a fellow parasitologist, and a contemporary of Rafe's at the University of Nebraska, where both had pursued graduate work. Glen called one afternoon to tell me that there was an unexpected vacancy in the group going to Baja California; an unoccupied seat was waiting for me in a rented van in California.

This sort of thoughtfulness is characteristic of Glen; he is simply one of the most generous individuals on earth; his students receive far more than they realize — incredibly detailed planning, bargain prices, instant attention to everything from a question about plants to a cut finger. His call to me was typical of his whole approach to life: I have something special, of value, to give to someone who I know will appreciate it.

When this opportunity arose, I dropped everything and got on an airplane for Los Angeles. Just like that. The only question I asked was of my wife: May I go? She, having lived with a scientist for nearly thirty years, didn't answer. Instead, she looked at me with eyes that said: If you have to ask if you may go to the Gulf of California for the first time in your life, then you must need to go far worse than you realize. A year later Glen called me again with the same offer, and naturally I accepted once more. *Vermilion Sea* is thus the result of two trips to Lower California, with a year of intensive study — geology, Spanish, molluscs, desert ecology — in between.

But my first visit was to be almost an impromptu one. The speed with which the opportunity was presented and accepted reminded me of some words of George Sutton, the teacher who inspired me to become a professional biologist in the first place: "Sometimes I prefer to send people out without any preconceived ideas." The people he was referring to were doctoral students; "out" usually meant to Central America; "preconceived ideas" applied to birds. Sutton was right. I have learned in the ensuing years that teachers get the most original work from their most ignorant students. Such idealism can easily be drawn upon to justify the fact that I was going to Mexico without knowing what the hell I was doing. Well, that's not entirely true; I *would* put my hands in Steinbeck's sea.

Technically my first trip to Baja California consisted of three weeks of travel with Rafe Payne, Glen Dappen, and seventeen university students. We stopped at various locations in the desert, winter birding grounds, the beach south of Mulegé, and a building in Bahía de los Ángeles that a man named George Lindsay, who directed field studies for the San Diego Natural History Museum, had christened the Vermilion Sea Field Station. VSFS served as our major base of operations. The name "Vermilion Sea" may have had its origin in the sunrise over Bahía de los Ángeles: Each morning the water is red for a very few minutes. Slides never do the scene justice; the colors are better remembered than photographed. Art historians have claimed that Joseph Turner, the British genius whose ethereal red and yellow swirling landscapes set nineteenth-century England on its ear, never missed a sunrise or sunset. Mornings at Bahía reminded me of the reason for Turner's behavior: that the most ephemeral of qualities — color over the ocean — appearing at fairly predictable times can give one a view of the world not available by other means.

Thus I found myself studying sunrises. My photographs do not show what I saw; they only suggest what I needed to remember about Bahía de los Ángeles the place and Bahía the state of mind.

This book is intended to be a sort of cosmology, an example of one way to see the universe. I have tried to write *Vermilion Sea* as an intellectual field trip. The subjects are not presented chronologically, like a literal travelogue, but in the sequence I became aware of them. My first impression of Lower California was of mountains, desert, and cactus. This impression is similar to that of a number of writers and is reflected in books ranging from the Erle Stanley Gardner adventures to Ann Zwinger's elegant natural histories. Beyond the desert, however, lies a shoreline that is a complicated system into which one is drawn slowly, with gradually increasing awareness.

Only after careful study of all these habitats did I begin to realize their true complexity. Eventually I saw the naiveté of my original intentions, and wondered whether I should reassess my dreams. I asked whether those dreams themselves were the important things in my life, or whether pursuit of them had showed me a world I'd never have seen otherwise. Thus it may not matter how close I got to a whale, or whether I found a brittle star, but that I went looking.

You will find little, if any, original biology, or "hard science," in the following pages. Instead I've tried to express the experience of a scientist who's done his ecology on the Great Plains, who knows this kind of work can be done anywhere, but at the same time understands that because of historical events, certain parts of the globe have attractions that cannot be completely explained by measurements and counts. Clearly Baja California falls into that category. Steinbeck's journey and book, Charles Scammon's discovery of lagoons where gray whales calve, and the building of a museum in Bahía de los Ángeles, for example, tell us more about values, attittudes, and world views than about how to grow food or cure an illness. So my hope is that this book reveals not so much about life in that part of Mexico as about the effects of going exploring in a charmed land.

John Janovy, Jr.

1

Thoughts over Colorado

What inconvenience attends my journey to see a whale, to simply see — before one of us becomes extinct — a live, wild whale. Like a funhouse mirror, the airplane's double window distorts the prairie landscape, the runway edge, a distant treeline. Chunky vehicles crawl under the boxed-in, covered walkways. Early winter sun reddens the Corten steel of the terminal building. Corten is a sculptor's material; it is supposed to rust, then stop rusting after a certain time. But nothing stands forever unless maintained, certainly not steel buildings nor species, not even a human mind. Thus I am on my way to Mexico to gather ideas and repair the damage of too comfortable an existence.

The runway asphalt is cracked from the wear and tear of weather and tires. That broad straight path across the prairie, where we launch ourselves into other worlds, shows the marks of age and use. I consider the possibility that experienced travelers can determine which city they are in simply by looking at the tracks on the runways. A friend once told me you could recognize individual whales by their scars — traces of their encounters with the physical world and places where the opportunists came to rest. So whales bear marks of experience, evidence that they've outlived their parasites, slipped past the edge of broken ice, left the reefs behind.

As the jet's acceleration pushes me into the seat, I wonder what it feels like to have a barnacle attached to your back, that will be chiseled off only in death, and only then if you are washed up on some beach and a curious person comes along gathering barnacles. In the West we consider scars to be proof that we've survived rough times. But if the world stays on its present course, the times ahead are likely to be rough beyond imagination. There is only one certainty, for both the cetaceans moving as dark shadows through a murky ocean and my companions on this airplane: Humans can't continue multiplying and drastically altering their environment, then expect nothing to happen to whales. So the time has come for me to see a whale alive.

The ground over which the airplane now rises also has scars: gently sinuous harvest trails through milo stubble, road cuts, circular center-pivot pox marks, the slashed-wrist open wound of a diked irrigation canal. These gouges are a record of our self-fulfilling prophecy that if we cut and dig, altering the landscape, then the world will somehow be "better," that the land grows food most abundantly when it is plowed, disked, treated with chemicals, pierced for water. But the language of a prairie is no more easily understood than the singing talk of whales. We like the land because of the traces we have put on it. Good, we think; we've survived. But it has yet to be seen whether we will last thirty million years, as long as the cetaceans did before we came.

Thoughts of whales somehow bring to mind coyotes. They too can be distinguished as individuals, but they express their singularity in feisty ways — the smell of urine, facial expressions, modulations of their howl, a home range, an almost joyful cunning, wits unlocked and let run wild, drifting banner of a tail, the tiptoeing, grinning, snapping up of a stupid gopher. Many of us do not like coyotes; we claim they are predators on our livestock. But I suspect the real reason is that coyotes seem to enjoy their freedom too much. They gather no barnacles.

It is natural, I think, for these two images — the coyote and the whale — to surface together. One symbolizes my history upon the central grasslands; the other, the lives I gave up when I chose to make my stand upon the plains. I gaze down at eastern Colorado. We have started our descent into Denver. An erratic line of canine tracks is a string of decisions made in light snow. I look to the hazy horizon over the mountains. Ahead in time lies a giant shape that will rise out of the blue darkness to greet my skiff. The tracks tell me who I am; my sense of what a whale might be tells me who I could have been.

The Sea of Cortés was, for me, a mythical place. But with a single phone call, it became real. The plan was simple: fly to Los Angeles, spend the night, leave for Baja California the next morning. The itinerary read like any scientist's: Days were identified not so much by dates as by animals and places. A Wednesday became "invertebrates"; a Friday turned into "whales." On one Friday in January I would see a whale. If nothing else came of this winter, I *would* see a whale. And if I failed to pay adequate attention, Glen would point one out!

I knew, however, that when the dream came true, I might not be particularly stirred. When the whale surfaced, I could easily be more interested in an enigmatic gull than in the distant dark and lumpy back slowly gliding under the lingering blow-hole mist. Looking ahead, I expected many days in the almost intoxicating aura of the intertidal zone, a close brush with dozens of desert plants, and a serious lesson in geology. By the time we boarded a whale-watch boat to guarantee Glen's promise, the anticipated thrill might easily be diminished by what I had already seen in the Sea of Cortés. And I knew that back home in the middle of a prairie February, friends would look at my pictures and say "hmmmm," but would be thinking, "That's all there is to lifelong dreams? All he wanted to do was see two V-shaped spouts, one smaller than the other, way off in the Pacific haze, then take a picture so he could come home and say 'Those are gray whales'? Why, we got closer than that in the navy!" Then, reading the thoughts on their faces, I would not say, "Great, then the navy is good for something." And by not saying that I would keep all my friends happy or, if not happy, then at least comfortable with their opinion that college professors, especially biologists, live outside the mainstream of humanity.

We follow dreams to validate our identity. By this means we can establish boundaries between ourselves and the outside world that intrudes upon us. Organisms that invade our bodies are usually repelled by an army of cells mobilized in response to the assault; thus we maintain our biochemical definition of "self." Ants accomplish the same task by constantly touching, exchanging chemicals, then attacking those pieces of the environment that don't taste like the home nest. We often repel ideas that affront our world view; concepts roll off our backs like raindrops from the hood of a well-waxed car. Nations identify themselves by continually seeking an enemy; "communism" maintains "capitalism," no matter how rapidly societies operating under each system evolve toward one another. A man who puts a dissecting kit in his carry-on bag alongside his binoculars, flannel shirt and jeans, plastic bags, vials, and watercolors, is claiming, in essence, that he is a naturalist, distinguishing himself from the dark-suited executives who board the same airliner. And when his ticket reads LAX and his destination is the Vermilion Sea, then you know this man is searching for a lost person, namely the wandering soul who sat on an orange crate beside John

Steinbeck and Ed Ricketts while they thought about "what good men most biologists are."

Denver's Stapleton Airport has always seemed to me an interesting place; the people scurrying along its concourses reflect the allure of posh ski resorts, the cowboy image, and the freedom, as well as the challenge, symbolized by distant snow-capped mountains. Unlike Chicago's O'Hare, where walk-up bars are packed shoulder to shoulder with high-strung businessmen, Stapleton is filled with vacationers, people who have chosen to go flying instead of being forced into it by their occupation. Laughing children, chic middle-aged women, big men in leather coats with sheepskin collars, parade past my chair. I wander through the gift shop; the shelves are stocked with brass belt buckles, Indian jewelry, and rocks — hematite, olivine, chalcedony. Throughout the mountains you find an appreciation for nice stone. In an hour I'll be over Utah. There will be no cornfields below; I will have left my agrarian society and entered the geologists' airspace. I study the X-ray profile of my carry-on luggage. Can the lady in uniform tell from the contents that I'm going to Mexico? Ticket in hand, I take a last look out the window at my plane; this machine has changed the way we travel but not the fact that we do.

Pilgrimages seem to be almost instinctive, or at least derived from behaviors now so ingrained in our species that it's difficult to distinguish between genetic and social origins. Of all the animals that migrate, we are surely among the most restless. But humans retain the influence of the geophysical habitat in which they pass their formative years. And often, it seems, we are drawn back to our childhood homes — if not physically, then mentally; if not out of love, then out of curiosity; if not by necessity, then by desire. Through such returnings we find out who we are.

Of all the traits that separate us from other animals, the ability to detect a pattern of symbolic events and then construct metaphors and allegories must be the most distinctive. This trip of mine is thus the equivalent of an ice skater's "school figures," those congruent figure eights done to maintain an identity, to establish membership in the group of those who can trace predictable patterns on slippery surfaces. Such drills are assumed to be practice for the more rigorous performance that follows; they are repetitions endured because they prove one has not forgotten "the basics." And in this sense all practice is symbolic.

In addition to being the fulfillment of a dream, therefore, this migration is also a return to the intellectual conditions under which I was born as a scientist, my school figures — freshman lab, teenage wanderings through brush-lined creeks where baby catfish hid. I go to Baja California to recapitulate my ontogeny, perhaps in an effort to understand my phylogeny, that is, to relive my own intellectual development in order to discover the manner in which populations produce naturalists. Such an experience might be of value to a teacher. So I will be a child — a student — again, in a blissful haze of wonder, in the company of grownups who tell me it's okay to stay that way.

I first read *Sea of Cortez* as a tenured faculty member, contemplating nearly thirty more years of a professional life spent begging for grants in a stark building with dimly lighted halls. I finished the book and thought: This is a story of what biologists *are,* not what they *do.* Steinbeck's words express what a certain group of scientists feel but perhaps cannot bring themselves to tell about, namely an inclusive, multileveled image of the natural world. Such people pick up a starfish and "see" in it properties, ranging from the molecular to the metaphysical, that others cannot detect, so they tell their students to read Steinbeck's "Log." The parable of a scientist and a novelist seeking invertebrates while a world war explodes around them is now a part of the scriptures of marine biology and, by extension, all those disciplines that mimic classical marine biology in their approach.

Today science and technology have the potential to bring about as much change in the human condition as global military conflict did in the 1940s. The most important domesticated organism of the twenty-first century may prove to be not a breed of cattle or a cereal grain but the intestinal bacterium *Escherichia coli,* which molecular biologists use to isolate genes of other species. Such manipulations may lead to the solution of problems once thought to be as intractable as earthquakes. In politics, the fax machine ensures that a nation can neither easily hide a military action against its own citizens nor rewrite history to serve political purposes. In physics, superconductor research progresses, seemingly inexorably, toward discoveries that could completely alter the world's patterns of energy use. And yet the human population soars, virtually out of control, toward that level at which we, though in possession of undreamed-of technical power, will be unable to stop our slide backward into a purely animal state; at that point the forces of nature will do for us what we refuse to do ourselves — namely, stop us from multiplying exponentially.

Buried deep inside this indescribably complex mélange of events and circumstances is my freshman biology class. Three hundred eighteen-year-olds sit in a large classroom, patiently waiting for the words that will bring them life, liberty, health, wealth, a happy marriage, and successful children. One cannot stand before such audiences year after year without struggling over the questions of what to "teach" and how to "teach" it. In the middle of the Grain Belt, where vast supplies of human ingenuity are focused on the commercial exploitation of corn, where one is surrounded by an intellectual aura in

which family, longevity, courtesy, deference, and fiscal re-
straint are the most valued traditions, this question is an
especially difficult one. All the "good" things, it seems, make
our global problems worse, for they increase our numbers,
delude us into thinking our present circumstances are permanent, and hide the typical human's life by keeping us
ignorant of it.

Perhaps it is time to seek what naturalists look for when
they go exploring, then return to my hundreds of students
after having looked at living organisms through inexperienced eyes again. The two people who are largely responsible
for my travels to Baja California, Glen Dappen and Rafe
Payne, both teach at relatively small private universities. I
suspect their sense of what is ultimately important in our
profession — the production of educated citizens — lies behind their invitation to me. They would never tell me directly
that I have been hanging around too many colleagues whose
main interest is grant money, whose greatest fear is of being
thrown to the lions in freshman biology. Instead they invite
me to take a field trip to a place made sacred by a book
published in 1941.

The airplane engines change pitch; a stewardess comes
through the cabin, picking up empty coffee cups. Below, the
Mohave Desert lies seemingly empty, like an unknown past
or an uncharted future. The person next to me is an elderly
woman; across the aisle is a young couple. I wonder if they
know how much their fundamental condition has been changed
by modern science. Most of us see only the end results of
technology — cures and commercial products. Not many
outside the molecular biology fraternity, or the administra-
tors who hope there's a mother lode of patentable processes
lying around in labs, truly understand what has been wrought
by post–World War II discoveries, either practically, in terms
of potential for modification of living organisms, or philo-

sophically, in terms of our answer to the question "What am I?"

Unlike the alchemists, the gene manipulators have succeeded in converting base materials into gold and producing an elixir of life, a commonly cited example being the conversion of *Escherichia coli* into a machine for producing human insulin. The "base metals" in this case are one of the most common bacteria on earth and a segment of DNA containing instructions for making protein. The "gold" is the money realized from the sale of the molecule. Insulin, the elixir, administered as a drug, allows people with diabetes to lead longer, more normal lives than they would otherwise be able to live.

This example is only one of many, and that fact has precipitated a headlong scurry after the biotech dollars that financially strapped academics think lie hidden, like Easter eggs, in the federal agency jungles. And my students, the next generation of senators and presidents among them, seem to have joined in the game. What has yet to be evaluated by the unrelenting judgment of history, however, is our innocence. Collectively we don't understand the methodology, yet we covet the product. The scientists are in possession of what appears to be witchcraft; they are much like painters, composers, and novelists — theoreticians whose strange ideas keep others busy trying to turn the new equations into power. The work of such people sometimes catapults them into the worlds of kings. But the creators' original domain, the one that they call home, and the one to which they must return if they are to retain their identity, is the realm in which they exist not as businessmen and woman, political leaders, or public servants, but as pure explorers on missions of personal discovery for its own sake.

As the landing gear clunks down over the Los Angeles runway, I think that the border to one such home territory, be it a physical one or an intellectual atmosphere, is south of San Diego. The kingdom of original biology is not the political province of Baja California but the land where writers get to be biologists and vice versa. And so I hurry away through an airport corridor, toting the tools of a nineteenth-century naturalist. I studied animals not for a particular purpose, but because they were, for some reason, simply fascinating to me. I studied them like a curious child, even as I grew into a husband and father and employee. Beyond the so-called life-long dreams, the pilgrimage to places where Ricketts and Steinbeck collected, the "school figure" analogy, the explanation for why I stayed among the coyotes instead of chasing after whales — beyond those easy cocktail party openers lies the real reason I wanted to go to the Sea of Cortés: It was one more attempt to find the innocent wonder in a world of exploitation.

2

Mosaics

———

Looking down on the plains from the lower stratosphere, where airliners fly, one sees mostly squares or designs made from them — a sure sign of agriculture. Watching the fields creep slowly past below, I'm reminded of humans driving tractors and taking out loans. But beyond the Rockies the ground shows relatively little evidence of development. Ocher bluffs and washouts lie naked in the sun, revealing the physical processes that have operated on earth since its formation: erosion, orogeny, fault-block tilting. And over Utah the people who intrude on my reveries are not farmers and ranchers but scientists who study rock.

On the ground in Baja California, during the drive from Ensenada to a beach campsite at San Quintín, the distant Sierra San Miguel, lying inland, seems like a preview of the encounters we will have later with mountains. The jagged horizon moves slowly past the van windows, changing colors in the passing afternoon. Catching the last of the setting sun, the mountains turn a soft pastel red before disappearing into the darkness. The next morning, shadows on the western slopes make the mountains gray, but by the time we turn inland at El Rosario, the colors have returned to the hills. Across the Rio del Rosario valley the eroded Cretaceous marine sediments almost beckon; they look as if they hold a rich array of fossils. I study my map and begin to get impatient; it is long past time, I feel, to literally get my hands on Baja California, to see up close how this landscape is built.

Inevitably, barren cliffs and layered stone remind me of my father, who was a petroleum geologist. Nightly after dinner he would spread his maps on the dining room table. He worked on large rolled sheets of glazed cloth; shot-filled leather bags served as weights to hold the surface flat. Making tiny circles with a drop-bow pen, he would trace contours of underground formations, using drilling reports to "look" far below the surface of Oklahoma. I used to marvel at the quality of his work; the lines were perfect and beautiful, his freehand lettering more precise, somehow more authoritative, than any printing in a book.

When my father died we sold most of his maps, but I kept a few. They are a reminder that given enough information, a person can reconstruct events that occurred hundreds of millions of years ago, even though the results of the occurrence may be deeply buried. But these maps are also an illustration of what I've come to believe is the most fundamental activity of science: the recovery of a pattern — a "picture" of the world — typically from discrete bits of evidence that by themselves may mean very little. Thus I tend to prepare for travel by studying various forms of art — often pictures that reveal how local inhabitants have seen their environments — even though the trip may be in pursuit of science. After my initial trip to Mexico, I immediately began planning to go back, and thus I turned to the geological literature, which I knew was filled with drawings. The first item I found was the report of the 1940 cruise of the *E. W. Scripps* to the Gulf of California; the opening monograph, by Charles Anderson, contained a foldout map that I promptly copied and stuck in my notebook for future use.

On geological maps Baja California looks like one wrinkled leg of a pair of skinny patched-up pants. The separate pieces of cloth, cut in a variety of sinuous shapes, correspond to surface features; different shadings and colors represent the ages and fundamental natures of outcrops — igneous, metamorphic, or sedimentary — as well as their secondary form: lava flows, alluvium, or tuff. As soon as we crossed the border south of San Diego, I began trying to reconcile the diagrams with the actual scenery. On the ground I couldn't tell exactly where the Cretaceous marine beds, marked on the map with diagonal lines, ended and the short-line-stippled metamorphic rocks began, but the road beneath our wheels was obviously laid on one type of formation, while the jagged, multicolored mountains to the east were clearly made of the other.

The scientific literature told me I would be traveling through a chaotic land, geologically speaking. My childhood memories suggested that the turmoil would be obvious only to those who knew how to build panoramic scenes from tiny fragments of color and texture. Regardless of what it revealed about Baja California, the Anderson map I carried also conveyed two general kinds of information. First, the surface of the peninsula was a mosaic in which patches of various design corresponded to features that could be found in the places specified by the map. And second, the pattern was intended to be unique. That is, if one added or subtracted outcrops or moved them, changed their horizontal profiles, then the map would not "be Baja." The two maps — Anderson's and the hypothetical, altered one — would, however, be equally complex, and to the inexperienced eye, equally valid.

If placed within the domain of art, the two mosaics would carry an identical message, namely, "Here is a series of shapes that need to be interpreted, reconciled with your feelings, and evaluated as expressions of the culture that produced them." But in the intellectual realm of science, one picture would be "true" and the other "false." Your membership in the scientific fraternity would ultimately depend on your ability to distinguish one from the other. I put the words "true" and "false" in quotes because in science, as in art, they are not absolute but relative terms. The Anderson map is certainly "true", and useful, on one scale, but very lacking, and useless, on another.

During the 1960s and early 1970s, R. Gordon Gastil, Richard Phillips, and Edwin Allison, with the help of students from San Diego State University and the Universidad Autónoma de Baja California in Ensenada, made a detailed reconnaissance of the northern half of the peninsula. Instead of Anderson's 8½ × 14-inch view of the entire leg of land, bound into a journal as a folded sheet, Gastil and his co-workers produced three maps, each nearly 3 feet × 4 feet, magnificently color coded, large scale (1 inch = about 3.6 miles), and exhaustively labeled. In comparing Anderson's map with Gastil's, I was reminded of satellite images taken at very different altitudes.

Both figures are mosaics, but they fulfill scientists' criteria as well as artists'; they represent surface features that can be located by a man on foot. But together these maps illustrate what scientists know almost intuitively, namely, that all natural phenomena, from atoms to Mexican mountains, are incompletely described. Anderson's map tells a general, almost global story, while Gastil's is told at a human level. Studying the latter map, I could picture the geologists and their students in the field, collecting hand specimens but thinking of crustal plates, pounding their picks into a cliff but imagining ancient subtidal marine beds. I can almost hear their voices in the arroyo; words like "fault breccia" and "conglomerate" echo through the washout; the sound of falling gravel tells me they're moving on, farther up into the canyon.

Thus these maps warned me that once in Baja California, I too would have to merge global with personal views in order to understand where Rafe Payne and Glen Dappen had taken me. I knew in advance I would walk across boundaries between different rock formations and soil types, yes, but therefore also boundaries between geological epochs and tectonic events. To an experienced eye these transitions are as clear as lines on paper.

This discreteness is the property that James Hutton noted in eighteenth-century Scotland; deciding that an explanation of it was necessary, he founded the science of historical geology. What Hutton saw in the schist and Old Red Sandstone beds near Jedburgh was an unconformity, a sharp distinction, not only between rock types but also between the angles at which the rocks were laid down. The sandstone layers were near the surface and roughly parallel to it, while the underlying schists were tilted sharply upward, so that the bottom of the sandstone cut across the planes of the lower formations.

Hutton's contemporaries considered the earth's basic structure to be relatively stable. Hutton, however, concluded that an older earth surface had been folded, the edge of the fold had been cut off — eroded away — and new, younger, rock deposited on top of the cut edge. Hutton saw process in pattern. I would be challenged to do the same. Discreteness, instead of continuity, is possibly the most pervasive feature of the Lower California landscape. Borders are sharp; cracks, seams, quartz veins, shadows, separate the colors and textures; structure mirrors the isolation you feel upon seeing a lone man walking along the highway, or one-room plywood houses scattered over a hillside. In the town squares, tiles are set into the sidewalks; park benches are decorated with ceramic plates; away from the main street, stones are implanted so firmly in the hard dust that they seem to symbolize lives equally as fixed. These features are in stark contrast to the obvious fluidity of the Southern California urban landscape I'd left behind.

Even a local mission is built of blocks carved, laboriously and individually, out of nearby mountains; no two blocks are exactly alike. I read the sign on the wall; this church has been here since before the American Revolution. My God, how old! I think. But like the "stability" of stone outcrops, that of this building is an illusion, produced by my proximal view of history. The Jesuits who started the mission were kicked out in 1767 — an almost volcanic event — and the Dominicans finished the building twenty years later. The geological word "unconformity" comes to mind; if I only knew where to look, maybe I'd see the physical evidence for religious and political upheaval there in the walls.

James Hutton saw a series of events in a static picture. His friend John Clerk drew sketches of a high stream bank with its historical record laid bare. In Clerk's drawings different rock formations are presented as distinct patterns of close parallel lines, dark blotches, and crosshatchings. Although he may not have been the first person to show geological features in such fashion, he was an early practitioner of the method. Today's scientific publications and surface maps use the same graphic conventions; the newest research still relies on communication devices employed when the science of geology was born. As we drive past the isolated ranchos — Arenoso, Santa Cecilia, San Pablo — I wonder what kinds of building blocks I'll choose to illustrate the lives and houses from which I'm separated by my cultural heritage. And how do I use these tessera equivalents to imply the processes that lead to, and maintain, discreteness?

Studying the Mexican countryside from the van window, I write notes, make sketches, and try to memorize the distant mountains' colors, realizing there is a possibility that my own narrative will be as fictitious as the map of a science fantasy novel's setting. During a stop beside the highway, I take out my magnifying glass in order to have a detailed look at Baja California. No forest obscures the rocks. The poverty of rainfall produces a richness of vision into the forces that shape the planet, from the microscopic to the grand. Desert gravel reflects the dynamic history written on distant hills: upheavals, meltings, recrystallizations. And while others look at the horizon, I put on the close-up lenses and lean down to within an inch of a boulder, focusing my camera.

"They must not have rocks in Nebraska," says a voice behind me.

"Not exactly like this one," I reply. There are not many places where you can see a chocolate-strawberry-swirl mountain with one eye and with the other, the rate at which magma cooled, in the crystalline structure of a roadside chunk of granite. The far ridges are mosaics; so is the boulder chip under a microscope. When I get home there will be time to study the world at both scales, then walk away from the lesson able to see crystals and imagine the mountains and vice versa.

This was not the first time I'd been in visually complex territory characterized by great heterogeneity. I'm not a particularly sedentary person; I've been to Taiwan and Oklahoma, spent plenty of time in New Jersey and Kansas, driven the twisted highways of rural Washington and Oregon, gotten a speeding ticket in Arizona, studied fog through the Mississippi midnight, ridden a cable car to the top of a Swiss mountain, and sat scrunched in a *petite voiture* watching the vineyards as one of my students threaded a tiny Fiat through France. All of these places *looked* like landscapes, however, whole scenes, integrated visions, their separate parts merged into one view.

But Baja California appeared different, in some fundamental way, from other lands. The discreteness was always evident, no matter what the scene. I looked at the mountains but found myself focusing on individual boulders. I took pictures of the coast, but they turned out to be close-ups of individual shells. My notes about the winding blacktop east of San Ignacio are mostly of road signs, single elephant trees, and one red basalt chunk out of the millions. Back home in the library I searched for information on geology, — especially surface geology — published descriptions, pictures, collection records. I found maps, but nothing that told me why this particular part of the world exhibited a visual character so unlike that of any other place I'd visited.

So in desperation I turned back to my own photographs. The slides resolve the question: They had none of the richness I remembered from the actual scenes. It's easy to blame such problems on the camera. For a year I worked on this puzzle — how to take a picture that showed the same thing as my memory. In retrospect, the solution was relatively easy; make sure the photograph contains distinct parts that the mind cannot merge into a single image. A rock must retain its identity. The individuals can be only partly subordinate to the whole, and then only at their own pleasure. That conclusion reached, I felt that some of the Baja California mystique had been explained; its origin was in the mosaic nature of the peninsula.

South of Punta Prieta and west of Highway 1, in the vast Central Desert of Baja California, lies a long valley filled with a cardon forest, thousands of giant cactus standing over miles of hard stony ground. East of the highway, distant multipastel mountains form a jagged horizon against the glaring sky. There are broad turnouts along the north-bound lane, with ample room for vehicles. But on the other side of the road the valley is more like a museum; its silent occupants invite neither your close inspection nor your touch, and the shadowed scarps appear painted, as if added to provide context for the nearby displays.

The students are eager to get their hands on the vegetation east of the road, but they simply stand in awe of the cardon-filled valley to the west. Baja California has started to communicate with these young people, I think; they must be paying attention. They stare up at a cardon trunk, shielding their eyes, or gather in tight circles around a spiny shrub with tiny hard leaves. A few begin sketching, making notes; others just gaze into the tangles, realizing for the first time that desert is not only picturesque, it's also very much alive. Rafe calls his group together to talk about biology. I wander off by myself, deciding to study the ground.

In between the galloping cacti with their fallen, rotted, and rooted stems, the vicious and aggressively fragile chollas, and the agaves arising from the red gravel like nests of bayonets, lies a bewildering variety of stones: quartz, basalt, granites; pure whites, umbers, and near blacks. Under a hand lens microscopic jewellike crystals appear; palm-sized swirls of gray-streaked gneiss echo the larger patterns on canyon walls. I walk on a few yards, then kneel to take a photograph, carefully placing my knee between the ubiquitous spines. As I focus, I realize that the first impression, conveyed by a single boulder and the distant mountains from which it came, is correct: The fundamental structure of the peninsula is repeated at progressively diminishing scales, from the easily visible to the small to the microscopic. No matter how closely, or from what far distance, I look at this desert, I see the same scene: Baja California is a mosaic made of stone.

At close range I discover the ground is desert pavement coated with desert varnish. The pavement results from the settling and packing of pebbles and crystals in and among the larger gravel pieces. Microscopic grains, weathered off the mountains and carried onto the alluvium, are eventually removed even further by wind erosion. Small stones then become jammed and locked into one another to form the hard pavementlike surface. Looking at this ground, I can't help but think of chance and purpose, and how these two intangible entities shape the environments through which I walk. No end-directed, teleological behavior placed the individual rocks into the pattern I'm seeing. And on a museum wall, few elements of chance entered into the decisions to lay tiles, broken glass, ceramic shards, into the patterns called "art." Yet some — not I — would be willing to kneel on the desert and claim "God made this," then walk to the museum, take affront at the polemic quality of any piece of art, even a modern abstract mosaic, and wonder aloud, "What purpose does this serve?"

Studying the land at a distance of inches, then sitting back to survey the great Central Desert fading, miles away, into low peaks, I'm struck by the power of wind to change the face of earth. Over vast time and space, the air has moved and made its art, upon which we can kneel with a camera. Without wind, and water, of course, we'd have no plains; without the underlying pressure of molten crust, no mountains, for the blowing dust and periodic torrents would, in a few million years, reduce them all to dirt. The distribution of colors and textures is the product of massive forces working against one another. So too, I think, sitting on the desert, are the pieces on museum walls, the great panels on public buildings in Mexico City, intricate patterns laboriously fitted into patio walks.

But the photographs of distant hills never show what I see as I kneel. The phrase "sculpted by the wind" is often used to describe the pedestals upon which rest, precariously, hard cap rocks of an archetypal American West. But the concept also applies at a much smaller scale. Pebbles wedged into the desert pavement tell a story of blowing sand and dust, of abrasion, and slow chemical reactions. And just as one must sometimes seek out an expert to explain a work of art, so I have to find a geologist, preferably a crusty, sagacious, no-nonsense field man, a practitioner of the arcane skill of reading stones, to tell me about my souvenirs from Punta Prieta. Back at the university, I choose Sam Treves, whose first love is meteorites.

"Hmmm, a ventifact!" says Sam, almost before I'm able to get the rock samples out of their bags. Laid out on his desk, they look forlorn, uprooted, a long, long way from home, migrant workers in the industry of my mind. "You can sometimes tell the direction of prevailing winds by the shapes and orientations of these faces."

He rubs his fingers over an angular piece of basalt, turning it this way and that and finally holding it for a time with the small end pointing east. In his mind he is reconstructing the environment from which this particular rock was collected. I can see experience at work; he doesn't need my photographs; a single small stone tells him more about the Central Desert than I have learned in a year. You're being unfair to yourself, I think, as he pulls out his hand lens and inspects another specimen. After all, he could bring me a microscopic worm and I could reconstruct the fish from which it came, or at least make a credible attempt at doing so. Then I think, we all have mosaic maps in our heads, all of us who study nature as a profession, and eventually we learn where many of the pieces are supposed to fit into the larger scene. Later I read about the use of ventifacts to infer something about the Martian weather, and I am not surprised at my fellow scientists' ability to perform this kind of feat using only space-probe photographs of an alien desert.

The small stones are not only sculpted, but also painted by

the air. In the desert, minerals at the exposed surface react with oxygen to form reddish iron and manganese oxides, which hide the underlying crystalline structure and disguise the granular texture of the rock. This surface coating can be used to estimate the age of petroglyphs — figures scratched into boulders by aboriginal artists. Centuries, if not millennia, may be required for freshly broken pieces of granite to acquire their deep red or almost black patina of "varnish." An abstract sunrise hacked into a varnished surface might be visible for hundreds of years, if the marks were deep enough to reach unaltered rock. If the design grooves are also coated, however, then they must be ancient, because the surface oxidations occur so slowly.

But such methods of dating pictures are inexact. In cases where we have a historical record, petroglyphs known to be a hundred and fifty or two hundred years old sometimes look as if they were carved yesterday, and when the desert varnish extends into the scratches, that age estimate may be multiplied by a factor of ten. Some archeologists suggest that the richest patina could not have formed under the most arid of present-day conditions, and thus the petroglyphs might date from the end of the last glacial period, several thousand years ago.

Only one side of my pebble is varnished. By inference, therefore, my collection of a sample for later study disrupted an arrangement of small rocks that had not changed significantly for decades. In truth, the years might be more easily counted by hundreds than by tens. I'm inclined to interpret such a length of time as evidence for stability, but in a geological sense all landscapes are ephemeral; change is perhaps the only constant feature of my planet. Nevertheless, a single varnished desert stone teaches me that I have the power, with only my fingers, to alter an ancient environment. And strictly speaking, in order to ensure that my mental map of Baja

California is correct, I should return the little rock to its proper place.

Like a tessera or a desert stone, my trip becomes a distinct and identifiable part of a life spread across a sheet of space and time. From a study of art and desert, I learn to build mosaics whose pieces are chips of experience, a skill that is not consumed by such use, but rather is honed and polished, maybe even replicated, in those I teach. Thus by analogy, I think, there is a time to do your daily job and a time to go exploring in places you've never been before, and both must be present and in their proper context before the mural can be considered complete. Standing alone on the Central Desert, watching Rafe and Glen with their students half a mile away, I realize I must do two things immediately, before we get to the beach and the intertidal rocks: handle a cactus and try to climb one of these red mountains.

3

Cacti

I decide I've squandered enough film on ventifacts, and cross to the ocean side of Mexico Highway 1. Alone in the silent valley I step around the dead agaves full of scorpions, making my way through the tangles of spines, searching for the image that will later, in the comfort of my living room, bring back the feelings I get standing among the countless cardons, each towering and massive, and each, it seems, watching my every move. Their bases, or "trunks," are so large I cannot reach around them; their green, ribbed arms look as if they would break off under their own weight. Vulture droppings make a whitish cap here and there on the tallest branches. I have come to study the desert, but I feel as if I've intruded into a land of old plants. Although they cannot speak my language, their spines and postures tell me to learn what I can quickly, then leave.

"Forest" is the correct word to describe this population of cacti; the plants are tree-sized, branching, their bases covered with thickened, barklike cuticle. Each is distinctive in shape, yet unmistakably a member of its species. Camera in hand, I study many individuals, thinking somehow that by capturing one of these giants in a certain way, I can collect not only the whole valley, but also the species. I choose my specimen and walk around it, through the tangles of cholla, looking for just the proper angle, background, shadows, and "personality" — that is, scars. I have no idea where big cacti get their scars, other than the ones, of course, written in Mexican slang.

I touch them all — the cardon, the *garambullo,* the *pitaya agria,* even the chollas. But it is the cardon that I come back to, running my fingers over the heavy gnarled base, wondering if this particular specimen was alive two centuries ago, then up the stem, between the ribs, over both the smooth and the rough places. This habit of touching is one I picked up in a museum, in a room called the Encounter Center. A sign on the door read "Please touch." So, along with the masses of elementary school children, I did. Now others may stand and enjoy the scenery, marvel at the desert beauty, subtle colors, serenity, and silence. But I must handle the cacti. They are not harmed by this activity, nor by Rafe picking their fruit and slicing it for us to taste. These plants do not talk or sing; we can see them, put their juices in our mouths, smell their flowers at some times of the year. And while their spines say silently, "Do not touch," this is the very reason to do so. In this way we can use four senses, instead of three, to help remember the desert. I pick a small spine out of a dirty fingertip and return to the camera, having found my subject.

By selecting one individual from the thousands, asking that it represent its species while retaining its uniqueness, I make one cactus the equivalent of a character in a novel. Big, challenged by a harsh environment, long-lived enough to have acquired a history, constrained by heritage and habitat, yet successful by virtue of its very presence before me, this one plant brings to mind Saul Bellow's bedeviled Charlie Citrine (*Humboldt's Gift*), or his driven Henderson (*Henderson the Rain King*). But by indulging in this mental game I only underscore the world of difference between art and science at the practical level, for when it comes time to truly characterize *Pachycereus pringlei,* the cardon, distinguishing it from all other kinds, the novelist's schemes fail, and the empirical mindset reigns.

Pachycereus was a name originally used by Alwin Berger in 1905 to describe plants, then included in the genus *Cereus,* whose flowers had short, spatulate outer perianth segments, numerous stamens inserted along the throat, and small scales, with felt and bristles in their axils, covering the ovary and tubes. Acquiescing to the inescapable reality of nature, however, he admitted that the very large, columnar, ribbed plants were "more or less branched." That is, he stated explicitly what we all know, namely that some aspects of nature are relatively fixed, while others vary almost indescribably.

Berger's use of the name *Pachycereus* was an attempt to separate, in a formal way, various kinds of large cacti from one another. That is, he intended to establish a history of nomenclature, in published form, that reflected his view of the cardon. And, as often happens in the world of taxonomy, four years later two famous scientists, Nathan Lord Britton and Joseph Nelson Rose, elevated *Pachycereus* to full generic status. Thus they acknowledged the seriousness of Berger's intent, as well as the validity of his biological decisions, and concluded that the cardon was not only distinct from other members of the genus *Cereus,* but distinct enough to have its own name. My experience with a long list of strange organisms makes me appreciate the work of these turn-of-the-century scholars. But at Punta Prieta, among the plants, I can see why a nonscientist might name not only the species, but also each individual.

"What is it?" is probably the most enduring question in the history of biology, asked by every student confronted by an unfamiliar organism, teachers trying to fix a pattern in students' minds, and any professional scientist who has discovered an interesting problem in ecology, or even biochemistry, only to be frustrated by the fact that he or she is dealing with an undescribed species. The struggle to answer this seemingly simple question has gone on for centuries. Modern molecular biologists usually resolve it by ordering named materials from a catalog, borrowing them from their friends, or making them in the lab. That is, they can avoid the problem by obtaining viruses, bacteria, and pieces of DNA that have already been characterized. Ecologists answer "what is it?" by wrestling with sometimes obscure literature and by constantly evaluating the criteria that previous workers have used to make decisions.

To those outside the profession, classification and nomenclature are at the heart of scientific esoterica, in the same category as disregard for clothing, love of crawly things, and other traits that mark the media's stereotyped naturalist. I often wonder, as I watch some binocular-draped character prance across the TV screen brandishing an insect net, what *should* this guy be interested in so he can rejoin the human race. Sex? Money? Power? Narcotics? Should he commit a crime or try to solve a mystery? If he is to solve one, is he better off as a cop or as a private investigator scratching away in dingy surroundings, trying to assemble a puzzle that requires him to view the world according to some skewed logic? Maybe we've come full circle; behind his beat-up desk in a cluttered office, our private eye looks suspiciously like the kinds of people who try to classify cacti.

Maybe our sleuth should encounter something beautiful to make his puzzle-solving escapades a little more interesting. Here the similarity between our TV character and his counterpart in the real world of taxonomy becomes at least somewhat real: To answer the question "how do cacti differ?" biologists turn to the flowers. This focus on blossoms reflects the basic way we distinguish kinds of organisms, namely reproductive isolation. If you can't mix your genes with a particular group, then you don't "belong" to that group in the biological sense. Flowers are sexual organs flagrantly displayed; fruits are evidence of successful breeding. In theory those structures used in reproduction should be the ones most likely to display features unique to a species. And cactus flowers, like their spines, are just another manifestation of what plants have made from leaves.

Cacti spent long centuries acquiring the genetic traits required to make both spines and flowers from leaves. But unless we know about this history, we think of spines only as defensive structures and flowers as reproductive ones, ignoring the paths they took to acquire their final characteristics. What information allows us to draw conclusions about the fundamental nature of spines and blossoms? The answer here is reasonably straightforward, although putting it into practice requires some skill and patience: We look for the evidence of what these plants must have been like before they were cacti. And within this answer lies some of the difference between scientists and nonscientists. The former know how and where to look for such evidence; often the latter don't believe it exists.

Vascular plants probably appeared on earth at least four hundred million years ago, during the Silurian period. We have this information because paleontologists are able to date fossil-bearing rocks through the use of radioisotope techniques and to cut those rocks with diamond saws into slices thin enough to be studied under the microscope. There we can see the patterns of cells built by living plants before the dinosaurs evolved to eat them. Although they didn't have leaves, these early land plants had tissues that functioned to transmit fluids.

In living plants, the movement of vascular tissue during growth can be traced by following a series of tissue sections through various stages of development. Thus, by studying how adult structures are formed, biologists can not only reconstruct a plant's embryological development but also infer some of its evolutionary history. Determination of fundamental character through discovery of the fate of parts during progressive change is one of the most commonly used intellectual tools in all of biology. In a previous century we used knives and lenses to discover that our heads were, in part, fused and compressed gill chambers. Nowadays we know, from using the same techniques, that cactus flowers and spines are both made from the leaves surrounding axillary buds.

At the bottom of the flower, around the ovary, wool grows from the areoles. In the case of the cardon, the individual wool strands are very numerous. The flower tube itself is scaly, and its areoles have a dense, feltlike covering. Species of *Pachycereus* other than *P. pringlei* display a variety of scales, ovary areoles, wool, and flower-tube areole structures. A naturalist always wonders about the relationship between species characters and their presumed role in the process of evolution. Thus we ask: If structural features are adaptations, to what environment has *P. pringlei* become adapted, that it should require, or even promote, the acquisition of dense short wool on the flower tube areoles, as opposed to the much longer wool of *P. chrysomallus?* Or what environmental forces are selecting for the persistence of wool on areoles all the way up the flower tube in *P. pringlei,* as opposed to the nonwoolly flower tube areoles of *P. gaumeri?* What is it about areolar wool that makes it a character that varies among species? What is it about areolar wool that makes it a character of cactus, *period*?

Not everyone is harassed by these kinds of problems; indeed there are people whose worlds are free not only of mosuitoes, ticks, snakes, scorpions, and cactus spines, but also questions about them. Such people go on vacations, look up at the heavens, and never wonder how the chaotic strange attractor equations might explain the red spot on turbulent Jupiter. They can stand on the shore and never see hermit crabs squabbling over empty shells, continental plates sliding apart beneath their feet, or mathematical models intended to predict how subtidal rocks, dislodged and rolled by an earthquake, are recolonized by tube-dwelling worms. They drive through road cuts and see only highway signs — speed limits, no passing, dangerous curves — not the earth's history revealed by tilted multicolored layers across the bar ditch. But the burden of the individual scientist is to ask questions — thousands of them, spread across vast space, infinite time, and scalar orders of magnitude. And for the biologist, one question tends to override all others: What is a species? How can I separate the uniformity imposed by type from the variation that is an inevitable consequence of individuality? That is, how can I pick the song from the noise? What is *the* cardon, as opposed to *a* cardon? Then I ask: Do the characteristics I have used for this purpose have anything at all to do with survival in the desert?

In his book *Metamagical Themas,* Douglas Hofstadter eloquently addresses the so-called letterform problem as it plagues the search for artificial intelligence. Stated simply, the problem is this: Before a computer can be considered "intelligent," it must be able to do what most humans do easily, namely, recognize a single letter of their native alphabet, presented in a variety of typefaces, even in fonts they've never seen before. To use Hofstadter's words, "the essence of A-ness" must be detected clearly and almost by default every time a robot sees anything that is intended to be an A. And by analogy, in order to "read" the desert, you must be able to do the same task you perform when you read a page, namely, distinguish individuals from classes, the "essence of cardon-ness" from the single plant.

A professional biologist uses this skill to describe new species and to concoct evolutionary theories about them. A species description is a highly formalized document that contains the results of equally formalized research. The published description is "knowledge" available to all who are educated enough to read the paper. Thus plants and animals have two origins. The first is an evolutionary one, which we usually think of as a slow divergence from an existing species, taking place over hundreds, if not thousands, of generations, and the second is a relatively instantaneous literary one in which the species enters the collective human mind.

A comparison of these two different "creations" reveals a rather formidable problem in perception, one that underlies much of science, namely the question of whether a species, or for that matter any classification category, is "real." Once described, of course, species become real in the informational sense, no less so than characters of novels, particular versions of historical events, works of music, and so on. They acquire properties that allow them to be manipulated in systems other than the one in which they originated. For example, once the cardon is formally distinguished from other, superficially similar, species, such as *Carnegiea gigantea*, the familiar saguaro, the cardon becomes available for use in theories about the manner in which cacti in general evolve, studies about the way desert plants adapt to intermittent moisture supplies, and research on the role large succulents play in the maintenance of desert animal communities. But while cardons exist in the desert, and would have if humans had never appeared, they don't exist in theories unless people put them there.

Diversity is commonly understood to be the product of evolutionary change in which descendant lines — parents, offspring, and their progeny — become progressively isolated, reproductively, from one another. Classical Darwinism claims these divergences are adaptive. They are supposed to be selected by environmental forces because certain inherited variations bolster an organism's chances of producing surviving offspring. Over long time periods, adaptations theoretically isolate a genetic line from its competitors, as well as lead to distinctive structures. But at a higher level — the metascientific — we question whether the underlying assumptions are indeed correct. Are we justified in assuming that all consistent differences among related kinds are indeed adaptive?

Another way of phrasing the question would be: What elements of the Mexican desert conspire to maintain species differences in the length of wool on flower tube areoles? Is this feature somehow related to pollination? But cactus flowers are typically large funnels filled with anthers that bear pollen and surround the pistil, containing the ovule. Nothing about this flower structure suggests they are linked to particular insects for pollination purposes, as some orchids are. On the contrary, their form indicates that they can't help but be pollinated, by bats, hummingbirds, a resting vulture, a shrike looking for a straight spine upon which to impale a lizard. So of all the features that *should* have something to do with reproductive isolation, the feltlike wool fuzz on a flower tube areole should be the least. But scientists use this character, as well as many others whose adaptive value is not obvious, to distinguish cactus species that in theory have each adapted to a unique environmental niche.

Standing in the cardon forest, looking down the long valley at the thousands of treelike forms, immobile and erect like silent green sentinels watching over the rocks, I find it hard to imagine a time or circumstance under which wool on the areoles gave one mutant cactus a reproductive advantage over another in competition for the Mexican sun. In a forest of giants it is hard to believe that the most minute details are also the truly important ones. The air is hot, even on a January morning. Radiation ricochets among the gravel pieces, gets trapped between the distant sloping walls, and settles into a wavering, uneasy blanket of heat. Nothing lives here unless it has found a way to keep whatever fluids it can steal from the haze that sometimes moves inland from the coast.

Of all the forces aligned against vegetation anywhere — shade, insects, dryness — dryness must rank among the most powerful. And so it is likely that areolar wool is just one more feature that functions to control water loss. The total surface area of all areoles on a cactus is no insignificant quantity. Throughout the plant kingdom, fuzz functions to retard the movement of air over leaves, thus reducing water loss through evaporation. This minute and obscure structural feature — areolar wool — occurring only at points on the otherwise heavy, waxy surface, might actually be a manifestation of the true dryness of desert.

The giant cardon suddenly appears vulnerable, if areolar wool is truly a defense against the Baja wind that may not break the branches but that can easily take the water from the thin place in the cuticle over the tip of a bud. When we use the structural details of an areole for classification purposes, we are really focusing our attention on the most intimate features by which various species make their peace with a harsh land. And so I find myself at the base of a truly stunning specimen of *Pachycereus pringlei*. Tons of cactus tower forty or fifty feet above my head. Thousands of similar plants, just as statuesque, dot the rock landscape that no longer looks barren but remarkably rich, complex, and diverse, much of the diversity supplied by individual forms of single species.

Again I touch the trunk, running my fingers over the heavy, gnarled cuticle. I look upward; the areoles I want to study are higher than my arms can reach. In the distance Rafe progresses further into the desert, stopping again and again, surrounded by young people taking notes and drawing pictures. I see him break off a cholla fruit joint, then cut it in half with his hefty fold-up knife. A student tastes the tissues inside. I leave the ancient cardon and walk to another one, whose spines are at eye level. There, with a magnifying glass, I study the largest species on the Central, or Vizcaíno, Desert (named for the sixteenth-century explorer Sebastián Vizcaíno). And later, back home, the pictures of areoles, taken with close-up lenses, are the ones that seem to show what I remember most about the cardon.

The name "cholla" sounds ornery; the plants that bear it look ornery; and even the briefest encounter with them reveals that they act in accordance with their appearance. Jumping chollas do not jump; their joints clinging to your jeans didn't leap there, but instead reveal your unknowing, and probably unthinking, intrusion into the space of a plant. Nor is a teddy-bear cholla cuddly; take this baby to bed and you have had your last good night's sleep. The chain-link cholla is not made of chain link, but a dense hedge of *Opuntia cholla* would certainly keep your kids and dogs at home. Only the buckhorn cholla seems to have been named appropriately. The word "buckhorn" suggests a Western landscape: horses, chaps, saddle holsters with lever-action 30-30 rifles, red cliffs, venison sizzling on a stick over the campfire. *Opuntia acantho-carpa* looks like a prickly set of antlers; from a distance, back-lighted against the setting sun, it could be mistaken for a young buck's rack in velvet. The pencil cholla, *Opuntia lepto-caulis,* also seems to have an appropriate name, but the story you'd write with its long thin joints would be filled with pain.

Anthropomorphism is a sin according to the prevailing dogma in the church of natural history, and an especially serious one among the fundamentalist brotherhood of pro-fessional biologists. We don't give nonhuman species human traits. The objectivist scriptures don't really address the re-ciprocal case, however, in which people are characterized by various zoological/botanical terms: dirty stinking rat, low-down weasel, couch potato, and such. Cacti provide great metaphors for use on humans: He's a cholla. No more needs to be said about this rapscallion. He'll use you if you let him; get close and he'll latch on for a ride to a new opportunity; brush him off and only later you'll discover his lingering barbs, too small to notice at the time but now festering. His scars don't give him dignity; they suggest a knife fight or motorcycle race instead of a noble struggle against insur-mountable odds. He clones himself with frustrating speed. Even his blossoms can be a lie, for some chollas have com-pletely abandoned seeds as a means of procreation. Their flowers are sterile.

The genus *Opuntia* is one of the most diverse and enig-matic among the cacti. *Opuntia* generally fall into two groups: those with flattened joints or pads (the prickly pears) and those with more or less cylindrical ones, the chollas. All are wondrously able to reproduce vegetatively. Joints break off and fall to the ground or stick to passing animals, to be carried as far and wide as a bighorn sheep can wander in an hour or a day, however long it takes for the pad to get knocked off. Then the pad takes root. Wood rats carry cactus joints and pile them into their tangled nests. Chasing a rodent into such a midden would be an act of ultimate stupidity. And once in a great while a storm cuts a narrow swath through the hills, washing pads down into the arroyo and out onto the alluvial plain, where they may put down roots and begin their asexual reproduction anew.

I duplicated this last event once in Nebraska, when I took a prickly pear from a Platte River sandbar that had become a permanent island, stabilized by invading brush, and hauled it three hundred miles downstream. The pad lay shriveled and brown in a flower pot of river sand in my office window for three years. Then one day, while providing the dead joint with its monthly drink, I noticed a tiny green stub, which enlarged slowly in the subsequent weeks. This kind of experience makes one view the magnificent Baja chollas with a certain appreciation of their potential age and, more important, their history, resilience, and tenacity.

In the case of chollas, disjointed rooting often results in forests of progeny surrounding a parent cactus. Through vegetative reproduction these plants can produce an entire population of clones in which one combination of genes is preserved and disseminated very rapidly. Asexual reproduction via abscission of joints guarantees that of all the billions of potential genetic variants that *might* have occurred in a population, an infinitesimally small number actually *do* occur. Some scientists assert, for example, that the present population of teddy-bear cholla may be a single strain that migrated out of Mexico after the last Ice Age and has occupied the deserts of the American Southwest for the last four to eight thousand years. Such contentions are backed by reasonable evidence, leading me, as I stand in the great Central Desert of Baja California, to wonder *which individual plant,* of the thousands I see, might be the progenitor. Which *one,* I ask, was the original teddy bear, whose descendant line of joints has survived eight thousand years, carried northward by wood rats following the changing climate and advancing desert biome?

Then a strange question appears like a distant mirage, wrinkling the scene, making it shimmer in my consciousness: Is the habit of making nests of cholla joints a technology that originated with a single animal, then was passed by teaching and learning down through the ages? And so I regard the mess before me: an ancient *Opuntia bigelovii,* surrounded by its stickery brood, and a nearby pile of joints heaped on purpose into an impenetrable mound, and I wonder whether this symbiosis between rat and cactus is the result of a singular event, one genetic/cultural combination that subsequently survived and spread across the searing, barren lunar landscape after the Pleistocene. Back when glaciers covered much of the continent and Baja winters were mild and wet and summers cool, wood rats made their nests of piñon pine and juniper trash — evidence of a more hospitable environment than the paved and painted desert. Starting eight thousand years ago, nests were made of cholla. Even the remote possibility that this change was the work of one rodent casts an eerie shadow over the scene before me.

Like the arrangement of desert rocks — varnished granite and wind carved basalt — the chollas now seem to acquire an air of permanence that contradicts their fragility and, in so doing, reveal the naiveté with which I entered their domain. I thought stones moved, and cactus lived and died like the rest of us. But this spiny, jointed plant, relegated to the blistering arid gravel reaches, is really an opportunistic survivor, a combination of extreme variability in outward appearance and an equally extreme genetic uniformity hidden in the nuclei of its cells. The very mechanism that promotes individuality, namely the vegetative reproduction that gives each plant its unique pattern of branching, strings of fruits, and scattering of clonal offspring, is also the means by which genetic variation is reduced. The unflinching brutality of natural selection in a harsh environment manifests itself in the chollas. A new genetic mix, perhaps as subtly different from its relatives as blue-eyed humans are from their brown-eyed cousins, lives or dies. But if it lives it spreads.

If we knew nothing of genetics, we'd be as mystified at our ability to distinguish cholla species by looking at individuals as we are at our capacity to recognize the letter A in its many scripts and roles. The letterform problem described earlier applies to chollas as it does to cardons, and indeed to all organisms. But we know more about the molecules of life than about the "essence of A-ness." The essence of cholla is an emergent property of cactus DNA; the traits with which our mind interacts, when we assign words like "teddy bear" or "buckhorn" to plants, are built of carbon, oxygen, nitrogen, hydrogen, and phosphorus. Some of us are confident that we could extract these traits from the cactus, put them into bacteria, then use the bacteria to make cactus juice. But what "good" is cactus juice apart from the cactus? It might be sold. Wonderful; now extract the essence of A-ness and insert it into J or K or X or Z. Can you make the Z express A-ness? And if so, can you sell the isolated property? How much is lingui-engineered A worth on the open market? In trying to describe the desert, I come to see my language, although briefly explored, still as stingy as the Vizcaíno with its secrets.

There is one last lesson to be learned from cholla. These are highly successful plants occupying one of the harshest terrains on earth. In the Central Desert average monthly temperatures range from sixty to eighty degrees Fahrenheit, with precipitation peaking at less than an inch per month in March and September. "The Central Desert has no dependable rainfall," writes Homer Aschmann in his demographic and ecological study of the area. An entire year may be completely dry. The area near Punta Prieta may be the driest of all. A wind that can produce ventifacts multiplies the combined effects of heat and dryness. Yet chollas abound in a wonderful profusion of individual diversity. If the population biologists are correct, that individuality is superimposed on a narrow range of the genetic potential available in *Opuntia* species. Constraint of potential at one level does not inhibit it at another. All nature demands of cholla is that the plants dispense with one kind of excess, and another is allowed.

Only in our minds does every mathematically possible combination of genes have a right to be produced. The actual squalling baby sucking its first breath is one thing, but the *idea* of an unborn, and unconceived, human is quite another. We have not learned this simple lesson, I think. We will lose our chance to be as wildly individual as the cholla if we try to ensure that all who might possibly exist do in fact exist. Nor have we learned our math very well. No earth can hold all the possible humans. Nor can any desert hold all the possible cacti.

4

Mike's Mountain

———

West of Bahía de los Ángeles, halfway down the Gulf side of Lower California, lies a rocky ridge known as Mike's Mountain, and north of that a great alluvial fan spreads into the bay. Bahía the town, seen from one of the bay islands, is a thin line of irregular buildings against the massive red backdrop. On the shore, houses stand in a boulder field, except for those closest to the water, which rest on sand. The sun sets behind Mike's Mountain, throwing Bahía into shadow, and the afternoon turns cool. To the west, beyond the tower and spine of *granodiorito,* lies a sea of *metasedimentaria.* This general pattern — uplift eroded into a plain at the foot, all glaring and naked, spreading into the ocean — is repeated throughout the peninsula. Mike's Mountain is only one of thousands whose granitic outcrops, folded recrystallized sediments, and mixed gravels are easily accessible to the touch.

There are scientists who can walk across these familiar formations, show you where the rocks have moved from their original positions, and use this information to estimate the age of the land. Geologists can easily determine where, along the evolutionary progression from uplift to sand, this particular range of mountains lies. In addition, the metamorphosis revealed by dark lines of schist, mineral traces through the gneiss, and the crystalline structure of hillsides as seen under the hand lens, tells them whether that progression has been direct or roundabout, meandering through the various physical and chemical options available to rock. To the trained eye, a landscape reveals the forces that shape it.

No less can be said of the array of patterns in living organisms — cardon, cholla, cirio, creosote bush, and the bighorn sheep among them — or of the inner landscapes through which our thoughts dash for cover or display their mating colors. Each scene appears static unless viewed from the perspective of prior knowledge — where we've been, which steps were upward, and which went around the obstacles. Then we can say, "This is how the universe is today," and the single word "today" is an addition so profound that those who can insert it easily and comfortably live in a world apart from those who cannot understand why the word is necessary.

The difference between these worlds is an ability to detect process in the lines and colors of a very thin slice of time. Baja California provides the opportunity to try your skills at this task, but you have to give yourself a few hours. My companions are ready to take the time; this morning we climb Mike's Mountain. I get to test my ability to "read" the landscape, and I come back down feeling as if I've finished a great book. The ground between us and the ridge crest looks like the sustained narrative of a major novel. The "words" are rocks, the "sentences" arroyos, and the paragraphs plant communities, mainly cacti and other thorny growths that long ago became stingy with their leaves. I suspect the distribution of plants is a composition resulting from the underlying mosaic of soil types, in much the same fashion as a chapter emerges from the constraints and opportunities its characters impose or provide.

"We'll walk that way." Rafe points to the bottom of the hill a mile away. "Then turn left. The trail goes around and up the south side. It's well marked."

Although the mountain is craggy in places, you don't have to be an expert climber, just a careful and persistent one, wearing the right shoes, to get to the top. Rafe is right about the trail being well marked. Previous climbers have left little stacks of three stones at various points. While these markers are more "natural" than a steel post, the stacking is nevertheless a rather blatant human construction in a rapidly weathering land.

But on the trail marked with stones, one also has to be prepared for time shock. I turn to look back where I've been; the forces that carved the scene stand out more prominently than the land itself. The years required for nature to wear away the peaks seem short because the effects are so apparent: Talus slopes lie barren below the fractured cliffs; small piles of pink gravel issue from deep cracks in nearby outcrops. Every step most of the way is like walking on a bed of rice, my feet slipping on granules whose origin is seen clearly in the crumbling pitted surfaces from which I can easily scrape tiny pieces identical to those that line the trail. Feldspar takes up water, then swells and breaks, sometimes in microscopic cracks, at other times in fissures that course several feet into the ground. We tend to think of granitic rock as solid, and of the desert as dry. The texture of the path does the same thing to my thoughts as the rare thundershowers and daily ocean haze do to stone, namely, rearrange them. This mountain is rapidly evolving into a plain.

The fine gravel is only part of the evidence for changes brought about by water. Here, lining a gully in the middle of a desert, lie trails of boulders as big as automobiles. I approach one of the few wide places in the path; the choice seats — those in the shade of an outcrop — are already occupied by the more experienced climbers, waiting for me to catch up. They act as if it's my curiosity rather than my city legs that makes me lag behind, although no one asks why I'm collecting rock samples on the way *up* a mountain. I take in the scenery; the south face of the ridge I'm on looks to be falling away into the chasm below.

"It's hard to imagine that much rain in this place," says Rafe, "but it must have happened." He has seen the raging flooded arroyos enough times, as well as the cars washed down into them, to appreciate the deluge required to produce this particular arrangement of stone. We stand and look at the tumbled stacks of boulders, the deeply cut gullies, and try to imagine such a storm, or several storms.

Like all rocks and ledges of a desert, the giant stones below make shadows in the morning sun. The strange and irregular lights and darks are an abridged version of what is to be seen in the hills north of Cataviña, where the boulders are so massive, and the fields so vast, that the dark crevices and glaring surfaces seem to be the thundering voices of the mountain gods themselves. But here the rocks that are not eroded to dust end up in the bay, forming part of the intertidal zone. There granite that was once high enough to be seen from twenty miles away lies covered with algae. Pelicans and cormorants drop feces on it. Barnacles and polychaetes build houses on it. Black porcelain crabs hide beneath the rocks, and starfish get wedged between them at low tide.

Standing a third of the way up Mike's Mountain, trying to communicate with the landscape, I suddenly remember two past experiences. The first began when a magazine appeared in my mailbox. Inside was a flimsy record of humpback whale songs. These wild sounds reminded me of synthesizers, steel guitars, harmonicas. But on the next track they had been speeded up, the effect being to make whales sound like mockingbirds. Big organisms talk slowly, I thought; if you want to hear what they have to say, you listen at their rate, not yours. Thus mountains speak in tones whose vibrations whip across the centuries, not the seconds, and only the knowledge of how the hills are born, live, and die allows you to "hear" this kind of language.

My second remembering is of a television script I once wrote that called for the narrator to seek out various people and ask them how they viewed the Platte River, what they personally saw when they looked at the wandering, sandy, braided prairie stream that flows out of the Rocky Mountains behind Denver. One woman he interviewed lived within the floodplain and had watched the river long enough to realize that of all its characteristics, the most constant was variability. She was intimately aware of daily light moods, the seasonal effects of snow in the mountains, and the strangling of the Platte by diversion for irrigation. She faced the camera, standing beside a natural valley nearly a thousand miles long, and said:

"Anything that changes is alive."

But beneath her feet the river was dying, bled to death by irrigation.

And down the side of Mike's Mountain the boulders lay washed, the soft fine gravel reflected its ocher waves, and the earth quivered. The hills west of Bahía de los Ángeles were alive, too, for the same reasons and in the same sense, as the woman's river: Both changed, progressively and irreversibly, from birth to death, and neither would ever be replicated exactly. Even a small mountain a college professor can climb has only one history.

I knew then why Rafe wanted to walk to the top — not necessarily because it was a challenging trail but because it was a metaphorical one. Each year he would see a more weathered landscape than he saw the year before, but he would see it from the perspective of added experiences, his own "weatherings." A seemingly minor afternoon hike became a powerful reminder that big decisions, like big mountains, always wait for those who choose to make them. On the way up, Rafe talked about his young son Luke and about the "right" time to take him on the climb, the age when a child is ready to learn that labor, fatigue, and inconvenience are small prices to pay for a view from the top.

To Rafe, Mike's Mountain represented a formidable task, not unlike the writing of a doctoral dissertation or the teaching of several hundred students in one class, and each trek to the summit reminded him that "formidable" was an impression, a property of your point of view as much as of the job at hand. It was a public mountain, made into a private one by Rafe's use of it. In that regard, I'm not sure Rafe Payne was much different from the Mike for which the hill was named.

Mike was a hermit; like his mountain, he had only one history, told in rather blunt language by friends who left a note in his cavelike shelter at the top. The note reads:

Please sign in — This is Mike's Mountain Merlin Milton Michael born 5/15/1915 Died 1987 in N. Dakota Lived and worked in Albaquerkie N. M. until he was 55, he designed the machine that made air filters for motorcycles. He lived kind of a loner lifestyle, never married or had kids. He served in the U.S. Army and rode a few freight trains in his time. Retired at 55 and moved to Bahia De LA. Worked on road to town for a while and then started exploring the hills. Built this trail over several years. He lived on Diaz property just south of town 1 mi. L.A. Times did an article on his 6 × 8 ft house back in 72. He carried most of the things in the cave up with some assistance from me. Don and Susie Campbell

The note ended with their home town in southern California. Later I called the Campbells to talk about the man for whom a mountain was named.

"He owned a machine shop in New Mexico," said Don, "but because of the competition, he got to the point where he had to either expand or sell out." Evidently it was not a very difficult decision: Mike sold out, moved to Bahía de los Ángeles, and lived off the interest. His first home was the shack; after a few years he bought a small trailer. He fished — he once hooked a marlin from his kayak — and hiked. He also drove his Volkswagen bus into town periodically, an act that might have led to his work on the road.

"He started by working on the road," continued Don Campbell, "moving rocks out of the way, mainly just to have something to do. Then he got to the mountain. He studied it, figured out the best route, his project for the day. He used just a pick and a shovel. When he reached the top, he dug out the porch, built the fireplace. There's probably still some water stored up there, buried in cans."

"Clothes bothered him," added Susie. "When he got to the top, he'd take them off."

Mike invited the Campbells to dinner. After that they started to worry a bit about his health. Don urged him to add some green vegetables to his diet of oats and food left by various campers, so Mike planted a garden of prickly pear.

"We ate the younger pads," said Don. "The older ones were kind of stringy. We brought him some alfalfa, which he'd sprout. And he grew some Swiss chard."

Michael's ingenuity is as much a legend as his trail. His backpacks, made from aluminum chairs, are "museum pieces." His mouse traps were highly effective. The homemade still on his trailer roof needed a continuous supply of salt water, but it yielded up to seven gallons of fresh water a day, plenty for both Mike and his garden in the summer.

Near the crest of the east ridge, overlooking Bahía de los Ángeles, we stop for lunch. The islands lie still in the bay far below; the alluvium stretches for miles to the north. The trail markers can't be seen, and the places I have been don't look the same from where we stand as they did on the way up. I ask Rafe Payne about the history of the trail.

"I've heard that it was originally an old Indian trail that he rebuilt."

An Indian trail? Who knows how many aboriginal feet or bighorn hooves had trod that same path in the centuries before Mike arrived at Bahía. Of all the places to go, and the infinite numbers of ways to get to them, why would the Indians come here? But then why did *I* come here, if not to see my universe from a new perspective? So even in the absence of a written record, I'm willing to believe that the earliest inhabitants of Baja California climbed in order to study the bay and the islands and contemplate the form of what must have seemed like the entire world.

The Jesuits who came to the Mexican frontier didn't record many Indian narratives about mountain scenery. Instead the priests taught the native Cochimi Indians the Lord's Prayer, then transliterated the aboriginal dialect into Spanish phonetics. Thus we know how a man from the Central Desert said "Our Father who art in Heaven," but we don't know how he described Bahía de los Ángeles from the top of Mike's Mountain, nor why he might have climbed the hills often enough to make a trail. Pablo Martinez, in his encyclopedic *A History of Lower California,* tells us that Indian speech was characterized by "continuous repetition of duplicated sounds, vowels and consonants . . . and differences were in the way these repetitions were made." When I read that, I thought: These people must have modeled their language after the hills themselves. Granite weathers; the differences among rocks are in the way the process is repeated.

According to Martinez, Indian commentary about the planet is preserved in some modern terms: their *caamanc cadeú,* a "reed creek," was the ancestor of *comondú*, the name of a geological formation, as well as of *kadekaman*, the town now known as San Ignacio, where the oasis must have been a reed creek before the missionaries' date palms spread through the valley. The name "Mulegé" evolved from *caamanc ca galaja*, meaning "large creek of the white mouth." I wonder about the word "white"; today the beaches of Mulegé are black, ground-up obsidian and basalt. The Indians called high mountains *idelibinaga;* the earth was *amet*.

Martinez doesn't tell us their words for erosion or molten lava, but from an elevated position, on any mountain, the Indians must surely have been able to see physical changes, even those of a geological nature, in their environment. It's entirely conceivable that the Cochimi knew about volcanoes and earthquakes. Some of the gulf islands — Pomo, San Luis, and Raza — are considered to have originated from eruptions less than eleven thousand years ago. Volcan Las Tres Virgenes, north of Mulegé, is still listed among the world's active volcanoes, and the city of Loreto to the south was leveled by an earthquake in 1717. But to moderns who learn for the first time as adults that vast crustal plates drift and smash into one another, wrinkling continents into mountains with the same abandon as rush-hour automobiles bashing fenders, the revelation can be disquieting. We tend to think of the earth's physical features as originating a long time ago, instead of being continuously formed. So I can't help but wonder what thoughts might have occupied the minds of a people who had little else to look at except the natural rock formations around them and who discovered that their planet was a highly dynamic place.

Were they frightened by the realization that mountains, the massive and seemingly indestructible constants, in time moved and washed away? If your culture climbs the rocks and tells stories, how many centuries does it take before you figure out that the sport fishing docks at La Paz are moving out to sea and the fake Gucci watches at Ensenada are headed north past Phoenix at the rate of a few centimeters per year? From the shoulder of Mike's Mountain, I look at Mexico through the eyes of geologists who have told me how the earth's surface behaves. This easily acquired knowledge not only affects my view of the physical world but serves as a symbolic framework for my perception of all seemingly permanent institutions. My climb up this rookie's hill has brought me to the top of a ridge, physically, and mentally to a gnawing curiosity about what extinct Indians knew, and what they thought about, standing in exactly the same spot.

The Cochimi had no means of measuring magnetism in rock, or the temperatures and profiles of ocean floors, no knowledge of the global distribution of fossil species. But they had eyes that were born looking at the landscape, legends, perceptions of the universe, and most of all, time — hours in the sun, decades in the desert. The question that haunts me from the flank of Mike's Mountain is: Which of the many evolutionary changes could they detect using only their naked human senses? How much can people find about the planet using only eyes, ears, fingers, and brains, and a language to pass along what they have learned? What does a primal mind do with the concept of irreversible change, with singularity, the idea of uniqueness? Have we gained or lost with our technology? The proximal gains are easy to list: increased longevity, sewers and air conditioners, airplanes, automobiles, satellite dishes, nuclear weapons to make us think twice before attacking an enemy who has the same. The ultimate losses seem abstract by comparison — a significant fraction of our self-sufficiency, a feeling that certain political events are beyond our control, and an understanding of what evolution, in the broadest sense of the word, means to one person.

Mike's Mountain lies near the southern end of a vast field of Cretaceous granite and metamorphic rock extending north-ward into the United States. The escarpments marching away to the east of Mexico Highway 1 were born a hundred million years ago, mostly from Pacific plate crust pushed into North America so far that it melted, then squeezed up through the overlying formations as vast plutonic batholiths, and finally weathered into the desert character for tourists to see. But south of Mike's cave the mountains are relatively young — middle Miocene, tens, rather than hundreds, of millions of years old — laid down as thick volcanic masses.

In 1940, at almost the same time John Steinbeck and Ed Ricketts set out aboard the *Western Flyer,* another group of men stepped onto the decks of the *E. W. Scripps* for a serious, seventy-eight-day scientific expedition, also in the Gulf of California. Among the second group was a geologist, Charles Albert Anderson, whose map I mentioned earlier. Neither as fulgent an idealist as John Steinbeck nor as blessed with literary skills, Anderson compressed the local manifestations of global tectonics into a few terse words: "To the west, only sandstones appear, and they grade eastward into volcanic conglomerates which in turn pass into tuff, and lava flows." That is, the closer you get to an edge, the more your en-vironment is shaped by fire. A new world of cleansing mol-ten stone rises up out of the collision of floating plates, each competing for space on earth, their momentum grind-ing up their borders and unleashing the fundamental heat it-self.

To the north, as far as I can see with binoculars, stability — Mesozoic granite — caps the landscape. To the south, up-heaval — an igneous revolution — consumes even the gravel washed to rest on coastal plains. At my feet the rock weathers into pea-sized grains, and a young cactus stores the winter frost until its pleats are stretched. The gritty soil around the plant's base tells me stability is only an illusion; a swollen succulent is evidence that a rapid response to atmospheric conditions allows the organism to persist in an unforgiving place. Tectonics offers a powerful conceptual frame to hold a picture of the grand forces shaping us, manifested as a massive collection of minor events. The crustal plates will never come this way again, I think. In the time it took me to climb this hill, the world has changed — forever.

The physical scientists — chemists, physicists, and geologists — address ultimate questions, that is, questions of origin, as well as proximal ones. They propose unifying theories, then seek evidence to confirm or refute their assertions. The science that gives me the power to interpret landscape in terms of process also includes cosmology — a particular view of the universe. And of all the unifying theories that might come to mind, that of the Big Bang, with its many implications, is perhaps the most inclusive. Where did all this come from? I ask: Guardian Angel Island off in the gulf haze, the ocotillo I'm using as a device for tying the nearby rocks to the distant horizon in my photograph, and my companions, now far ahead and above, well on their way to the top. Science answers: Once upon a time a point of infinite energy blew up, and all that is or ever will be, including the far and near, the stone by your knee and your friends up the hill, evolved from the debris.

The only problem with cosmologies is that, like crustal plates, they crash into each other. Perhaps the most persistent, and pervasive, collision of our time is that between science and religion, that is, between world views that depend on telonomic processes and those that rest on teleological ones. In the former, initial or boundary conditions dictate the nature of subsequent events; for example, the microscopic structure of granite, established by its rate of cooling, determines the size and shape of cracks. In teleological worlds, end-directed behavior, or purpose, plays a key role, as when we decide beforehand to go to Mexico *in order to* learn something new about plants, animals, and rocks.

If you accept the Big Bang theory, you also implicitly accept progressive entropic change, that is, evolution. Conversely, if you view humans as somehow unique in the cosmological rather than the biological sense (as a species distinct from other primate species), then you are probably not comfortable with the idea that our existence has no purpose, that it is the product of a purely earthly progression of life that didn't necessarily have to include us. But humans rarely *do* anything without a purpose; most of our behavior is teleological, even though we are not always aware of the ends to which we commit our actions. This trait may explain why it is so difficult for us to imagine that we have no reason for existing other than that the molecules fell into a particular arrangement early on, and millions of years later the matings went a certain way until some prehuman animal was committed to a trajectory of change from which there was no turning back. Such ideas are akin to the scientists' explanation for mountain ranges: Two plates ran into one another.

On the other hand, purposeful behavior may be one of the evolutionary accomplishments that greatly widened the distance between ourselves and our closest relatives. The need to ascribe a purpose to our existence might be a natural consequence of a hypertrophied end-directed behavior. For example, in a large group of structurally similar, freely interbreeding primates, the ability to plan a week in advance might be of enormous selective advantage. A subhuman who could decide on Wednesday that by Sunday he would have accumulated two handfuls of sharp rocks should, in theory, be a wizard compared to his friends who didn't even realize there was a Sunday, especially if sharp rocks were the limits of his society's technological advancement. To the other members of his clan, our prehuman would appear to be able to predict the future. He would *know* that by the time the sun went down four times, he'd have a big supply of tools. In fact, with his extended purposefulness, our wizard would not have predicted the future, he would have *made* it.

The preponderance of scientific evidence, the vast bulk of it gathered by those who believe falsifiability is the only valid criterion for a scientific statement, shows that evolution is the rule throughout the universe. It is the rule not only for plants and animals but also for galaxies, stars, planets, and continents. All have a birth, a period of change, and a death. To think that we can exclude ourselves from this universal fate is, of course, an act of grandiose arrogance, at worst, and a demonstration of the incredible power of mind (apparently) over matter, or myth over observation, at best. But to include ourselves among the other constructs of the universe demands an almost inhuman willingness to accept a position that has no purpose beyond that afforded the smallest beetle, namely, as a member of a community of species occupying a particular habitat. There are, of course, few better places to contemplate one's insignificance than very high ground.

The problem is that of uniqueness: How does an individual, as opposed to a species, construct a life? At present there are five billion or so answers; there are more people than mountains on earth, and their numbers may double or even triple in the easily foreseeable future. If you ask a New York advertising executive whether he'd trade places with a Mexican auto mechanic, the answer, most days, is no. The dark kid in worn jeans, smoking, drinking a beer, and talking with his friends through the open hood of a 1975 Ford at ten on a Sunday morning doesn't seem to have a "life." Yet if you ask the reverse question of the mechanic, he would look at you as if you're evidence of a *gringo* craziness so preposterous the local dialect cannot accommodate its description. If every solution to the problem of living out your allotted time is valid, then there is no single solution. The verbal paradox is as intractable as the natural one in which you can have a wild bird only by letting it go free: There is no right way to exist, only the way we each do it. And there is no best mountain, only each mountain. And the next one, or one hundred or one thousand, that arises out of the tectonic collisions will also be unique and will have as individual a history of weathering and erosion as the one you chose to climb.

5

Sacred Places

$\int$ome parts of this planet have the power to mold that portion of us which is strictly human, as opposed to "animal," namely our minds. These spots are not necessarily beautiful in the usually accepted sense, but they share one characteristic with the best abstract art: Their edges, shadows, colors, and color values communicate with us. The messages are enigmatic, with elements of both stability and change. Visits to such areas make us realize that printed pages are only combinations of lines and shapes and that regardless of what the words say, our imagination supplies the true meaning. Then the arrangements of rocks become equivalent to books and newspapers. When we are ready to believe this analogy, we are ready for a purposeful visit to a sacred site, knowing full well the experience may change us forever. Such a place lies just north of Cataviña.

"Lunch time," says Rafe, pulling his van off the road.

A permanent stream crosses the highway. Primal cultures in arid lands inevitably, and necessarily, have a relationship with dependable freshwater supplies that borders on the religious. We may be coming full circle in this regard. Throughout the arid West, in matters of "water resource development," rationality is often subordinate to belief. Computer-model predictions of basin runoff are read in as many ways as the Old and New Testaments, and the printouts arc used to support an equal number of sometimes conflicting assertions. But the shallow creek in this Cataviña arroyo, winding through the broken and tumbled hills, gives the impression of being little changed from the time a thousand years ago when Cochimi Indians must have sipped from it. To a casual observer the stream is dead. I look for endangered species of killifish, typical of isolated desert water, but I find no fish of any kind. I turn over a stone: no worms or insects. Life is sparse even in the water. The gravel bars grind and squeak underfoot; their grit is light and airy, fragile, soft, compared to the hard sands washing down from the Rockies.

No lush valley spreads out on either side of this stream, no vast alluvial plain, no rich silt agriculture, only stone. And such stone! The boulders stand head high and taller; they're coarse and grainy to the touch; my feet slip easily on their surfaces, sending small showers of particles into narrow crevices. Fault-block tilting, volcanism, erosion, are the forces we usually invoke when discussing scenery. These processes build the visual identity of whole regions — "The West" is only piles of silicates and minerals made by and from tectonic events. Yet here, north of Cataviña, is the real domain of boulders. And although I know how hills and ledges come into being, I can never quite reconcile this knowledge with what I see. Tell me, how can only the movement of continental plates, the torrential rains and screaming winds, the flowing intrusions of magma, and the crystallization of molten rock build this kind of environment?

We climb up through the crevices, stopping to take pictures, study the landscape, and imagine ourselves in a prior

millennium. We've come here to study designs on the ceiling
of a shallow cave, paintings estimated to be a thousand years
old. American students get to lie on their backs in the cramped
space and by dim light make notebook sketches of the yellow
and red figures on the rocks above their heads. Then, reflecting on the reasons for making such images, we try to be
logical: These symbols were used in religious ceremonies,
they mark the major social events of a culture, they represent legends guiding the footsteps of a wandering people, and
so on. Glen Dappen contributes the infinite particulars his
eye seems to gather continuously; he has seen more detail
in three minutes than most of us would in a week. Even
months after our visit to Cataviña, he will remember specific marks, their placement and colors. Outside the cave,
students' questions flow; Rafe Payne answers with questions
in return.

While listening to the seemingly extemporaneous, but in
fact exquisitely planned, seminar, I try to remember the vast
amount of art I've seen — viewed by choice, by accident, and
by virtue of being married to the education coordinator of a
major museum. Then I try to recall various experts' assess-
ments of this work — the lectures, slide shows, tours, whis-
pered critiques at wine and cheese receptions, late-night arguments conducted over the remnants of a private dinner for
six or eight. "Why was this piece done?" is a question we ask
of old paintings and sculptures; "what is he saying?" is aimed
at the new; and "how much is it worth?" or "was any public
money used to buy it?" is what we hear from senators.

Today all three questions apply to the works on the Cataviña cave ceiling, but I doubt they were asked at the time the
paintings were made. I sense that not only the artists but the
entire society knew exactly why the images were made and
what they "said." And nobody questions expense when all

agree that a culture must have a particular artifact — even a painting, I hope — in order to survive.

The sacred places of the world, those landscapes that shape lives, are routinely decorated with art. The patterns of scenery speak to us, and we talk back in the same kind of language. The Platte River of Nebraska, for example, and Interstate 80, which parallels it, are physical features that have directed the cultural evolution of a society. The people admit this overriding influence by declaring the river and its highway places worthy of art. Along the interstate, at rest stops, are monumental abstract sculptures. So when Rafe asks why people painted abstract figures on cave walls a thousand years ago, I look out to the horizon and see the answer: Here is where the scenery talks; here is where mind and earth exchange points of view; this is the land from which our culture is made, both literally and figuratively.

Travel through a picturesque foreign country often leads us to landscapes that seem to have enormous power because of their strangeness. But in truth sacred places are often quite mundane. Standing beside the cave paintings at Cataviña, I'm reminded of the physical location that has influenced my thinking more than any other — a nondescript and almost nonexistent river near an equally undistinguished, and indeed unincorporated, settlement named Roscoe, Nebraska. The only groceries in Roscoe are at a two-pump service station and consist mostly of beer, pop, crackers, corn chips, and candy. Sunlight glares off the grain elevator, but a stand of giant cottonwoods keeps the town in shadow. A quick glance down one of the gravel streets reveals an abandoned car and a small, well-kept house. Big news in Roscoe is a train derailment, an infrequent but nevertheless familiar occurrence. In the nearby river the water goes up and down, mainly down.

A student of mine was studying tapeworms in the toads

that lived along the banks of the South Platte River, and I also seined fish there for my own research. When we asked a local rancher for permission to use his land adjacent to the river, he issued us a key to the property. "Roscoe" took on a meaning for us that went far beyond its use as a town name; the word came to symbolize research — that rather bland term for the all-consuming intellectual activity to which a typical scientist commits his or her soul. Roscoe thus became a sacred place, the site of rituals by which we maintained our high spirits and a sense of purpose: the catching of toads and fish.

"This is my study area," each of us said, which meant we farmed it for mental sustenance. We "planted" ideas, approaches to biological problems, decisions about which observations to make, fertilized the germinating memes with insight and experience, and in the end harvested raw data — intellectual commodities that we then processed into publications. We marketed the products in exchange for admission to medical school, pay raises, and reputations. The sum total of this work established our identity. In a symbolic but nevertheless very real sense, we were born again as adults by our science, from the water and sand of Roscoe. Such creation evoked the same wonder as a germinating seed, the same sense of mysterious forces at work to guide our lives. When my student received his graduate degree, I gave him an album of photographs entitled "The Road to Roscoe." He could return to his place of intellectual birth any evening, in any town.

Humans are, of course, quite capable of being "born" any number of times. Initially, birth parents commit themselves in ways that are not only biochemical but also metaphorical. In addition to her genes, the mother provides molecules from which muscles, bones, blood, heart, liver, hair, and eyes are literally made, while the father provides "only information," that is, half the necessary DNA. When the intimate molecular interactions of the womb come to an end, the "making" of a child by its culture begins. The shapes of our buildings, patterns of our fields, flow of our highways, laws and policies of our governments, religions, and economic systems, having relinquished control over human development for only a short time — gestation and early months — return to the job collectively, with a vengeance.

Much of the so-called nature/nurture controversy rests on the observation that cultural forces are enormously powerful, as well as rather obvious and pervasive, while gene expression is hidden deep in the cytoplasm. Thus it is quite easy to say "she has sinned," because that statement acknowledges the power of culture, or "he has his mother's eyes," because such an observation, while admitting of biological control of a trait, ascribes no serious social function to that characteristic. It's not quite so easy to say "he has his father's tendency to be a schizophrenic alcoholic," because that contention mixes innate and cultural "causes" in a way that implies biological control of socially unacceptable behavior. We are not always willing to acknowledge the power of factors beyond our control; we don't want to believe that problems might vary significantly in their difficulty depending on their source, moral problems with biological origins being the most difficult of all to solve.

Beyond the physical environment against which our genetic traits are displayed, humans encounter the secondary influences of formal education, role models, and indirect effects of values and attitudes. Musicians, athletes, artists, and staff officers, for example, are often "made" from opportunities that arise, avenues of escape from whatever strictures are shaping a person. Sometimes these "birth" events are recorded. For example, George Orwell is said to have been "born" on January 8, 1933, with the publication of his book

Down and Out in Paris and London. On January 7 George Orwell had been Eric Blair. But there is also a possibility that he was "born" in the summer of 1936, when his narrative style changed from journalism to social polemics in the middle of *The Road to Wigan Pier,* a metamorphosis that eventually led him to write *Animal Farm.*

As in Orwell's case, a person's postnatal reconstruction is sometimes expressed as art or literature built upon, and transmitting, ideas. These products do not merely entertain, they also teach us to see the world in a particular way. That vision suddenly uncovers scenes, relationships, situations, to which we were previously blind. We ask how many of our preconceptions bear reevaluation; our answers sometimes lead to reexamination of values and motivations, and ultimately to changes in behavior. Encounter with powerful landscapes, be they natural or built by people using words and paint, thus helps us make the connection between ideas and actions, between thoughts and deeds.

Standing near the cave entrance, looking out over the distant boulder fields, I wonder whether the capacity to stimulate new ideas may be what sets the Cataviña arroyo apart from a thousand other washouts. Most elements of aboriginal sustenance were relatively widespread: cactus fruits and seeds, an occasional bighorn sheep, bird eggs, crabs and mussels. Of course in a desert, permanent fresh water establishes a location as a vitally important place, but there is no geophysical requirement that a spring lie in a visually imposing environment. At Bahía de los Ángeles the spring is as mundane as the next crack in the mountain; at San Ignacio the river valley clogged with Jesuits' date palms has green pools, an occasional snail, and the slippery path of fallen fruit squashed underfoot into powdery soil. But at Cataviña the water seeps from desert and flows into desert.

Heat waves rise from the simmering rocks and make rip-

ples in the mirages. Cardons and *garambullo,* the crested cereus or old-man cactus, stand among the boulders as far as I
can see, irreplaceable elements of a scene, still yet alive, silent
though humming with messages, blind but watching. These
plants are inaccessible inhabitants of a spiritual land, the ghosts
of shamans, or maybe of the few who learned a secret, perhaps by accident, then passed the knowledge around so that
all could live another day, another year. I can hear them talk
if I listen, but my shout back is lost in the rocks. Then they
tell me to make a picture; I obey the command, producing a
small drawing of a tall cactus against the distant hills.

Balanced on the boulders, looking west, downstream, lift-
ing my view to include the mesas marching away into changing shades of purple toward the Pacific Ocean, I am reminded
of all the times and places in which new ideas suddenly
appeared in my research program. Inevitably I was away from
my desk or laboratory, usually far from a telephone. Some
ideas were born of anger and frustration; for example, the
costs of doing biology and the rules and policies surrounding
animal care produced a vow to make computer parasites and
computer fish and mix them together in an electronic version
of my Sacred Place at Roscoe. For no other reason than to
escape the pressures of real life, I decided one day, walking
the South Platte River, that science and art could be effec-
tively merged in a place — the land of the mind — where no
one could pass a law, and numbers on a phosphorescent
screen could substitute for sand grains washing to the sea,
microscopic worms in mud, and striped fish darting through
the shallows. I sat down at a computer to make my mental picture come "alive." That image of the South Platte
River began FOR I = 1 TO M1:P$(I) = "M":NEXT. The
fish became FOR I = 1 TO 24:CN = INT(RND*(700)): IF
P$(CN) = "M" THEN M = M + 1 . . . etc. . . . :NEXT. The
anonymous peer reviewers of American science agreed that

my abstract vision of the river and its inhabitants behaved enough like the real thing to merit publication.

Years later I reread those theoretical papers, now depersonalized by time, space, and the formality of Baskerville type. Hundreds of people had taken them seriously enough to ask for reprints. But none of those fellow scientists knew that the papers had originated when I had looked at a river and been stimulated by a combination of stress and beauty to "draw" some abstract figures.

North of Cataviña, high among the rocks, it is my turn to wriggle into cramped quarters under the overhang, adjust my camera for the dim light, snap a few pictures, then sketch the paintings in my notebook for future reference, knowing that photos taken in caves don't always turn out. The difference between the scene outside across the arroyo, and the thousand-year-old figures on the rock ceiling is as great as that between Nebraska's South Platte River and the computer programs published in the *Journal of Theoretical Biology*.

Rafe asks his students what the Cataviña paintings "mean." The young people speculate, not realizing the width of the gulf separating nature from its abstractions. They guess "religious symbols," but their experience with religion is largely confined to that of the present-day industrialized world, and most of what they see in church is obviously representational. A few suggest the designs were medicinal, used as part of "prayers" for return to good health. They discuss initiation rites but don't specify exactly what role abstractions on rocks might play in these ceremonies. Personally, I think this last guess may be closer to the truth than they realize.

For the scientist, acquiring the capacity to use the appropriate symbols is as much a part of the initiation rites as learning how to operate analytical equipment. Today the sophistication of an area of biology is often measured by the stage at which abstraction substitutes for reality. For example, in order to describe a new species, we collect specimens, prepare them for observation, study them — often using lenses — and draw pictures, frequently aided by a "camera lucida" that apparently superimposes a microscopic image on a piece of paper. This illusion allows us to trace the image on paper. As a metaphor for the requisite intimacy between a naturalist and nature, the camera lucida has few equals; I peer through a microscope and there, in the field of view, is the point of my pencil. When I use the hallowed phrase "drawn with the aid of a camera lucida," the anonymous peer reviewers take it on faith that my picture is an accurate representation of nature. The words "drawn freehand" get the manuscript promptly rejected by the learned journal, no matter how superb the artistic talent masquerading as scientist.

But regardless of the accuracy of a figure, the precision of measurements, or the thoroughness of the statistical analysis, a biochemist could quickly convert my specimen into graphic argot whose relationship to the original material is so obscure I would have to be a member of the clan to believe that the abstraction represents anything from nature. The chemist might well pass off my original drawing as "descriptive," as opposed to "experimental," science. And through a thousand subtle messages, from tones of voice to grant support — the paralanguage of intellectual politics — I would be told that "descriptive" work is classical, old, and probably outdated, a low-level, easy, almost pretend kind of science, while the molecular machinations are "real," important, significant research. I often wonder what it is about science as a general activity that makes us value abstraction as a measure of sophistication.

There is a yellow drawing on the rocks above my head, a curved, inch-wide line with various rays, and next to that are some red ones, more "meaningless" than the yellow. None of these figures can be described in words, for to do so would be to attach meaning to them. Saying "like a sunset" would imply that the artist intended the painting to be a sunset. Beneath the granite overhang, in the noonday semidarkness, I think about bacterial chromosomes, wonderfully loopy structures, reduced to circles with coded, concentrically arranged, labels. Then I imagine rows of dark blobs, which are actually proteins migrating through an electrically charged gellike sheet, a step toward their purification. A whole stream of stylized, formalized, accepted figure types then flashes through my memory: the biologists' cladograms, Western blots, Southern blots, densitometer tracings, elution profiles, pulsed field electrophoretic mobility migrations, dendrograms of evolutionary distance revealed by DNA hybridization studies, and the geologists' slip and thrust fault diagrams, magnetometer records, and patterns of polarized light shining through thin sections of metamorphic rock.

Scientists have converted the natural world into symbols, then built a language with which to talk about them. We have measured the importance of our science by the distance between the figures and the language, on the one hand, and the plants, animals, and rocks they are supposed to represent, on the other. Finally, we have come to have such reverence for these abstractions, and the liturgies that surround them, that science mimics religion, daily research a form of ritual worship, late-night headaches our tithe to the Great Grant God in Washington, and a sojourn into some slumlike auditorium filled with three hundred freshmen our missionary service in the developing land of the eighteen-year-old mind. These are the thoughts about my profession that Baja California cave art inspires.

I have seen patterns, not unlike these above my head, in technical monographs. I accepted them, there on the slick page, as evidence of legitimate human endeavor aimed at the solution of some very difficult problems. Now I wonder whether the Cochimi might have made the same use of these ocher figures. The connections between real organisms and the biochemical "pictures" of them, for example, are the property of an exclusive scientific priesthood. Yet the modern lab wizards bring back to their public a formidable array of highly specific and often quite powerful entities — new compounds, patentable processes — finding instant utility in the fields of medicine, agriculture, and, of course, business. And so, staring at the paintings, I toy with the idea that these symbols, too, are the marks of those whose insight, mental and physical struggles, and discoveries provided their fellow Indians with products and procedures that were of use in the medicine, agriculture, and business of pre-Columbian Mexico.

Such speculations are a luxury of ignorance. The figures could be graffiti as easily as science or religion. What makes me think that just because aboriginal art is a thousand years old, it must be vitally important in some way? This beautiful, almost emotionally convoluted drawing could be saying, simply, "cacti suck" in response to a cholla spine buried in a swollen infected toe. The paintings could be on the rock shelter ceiling simply because such a location has protected them from the weather, the other banalities outside, exposed, having been long ago washed away down the arroyo, where Rafe Payne swears he saw a Porsche go tumbling in a flash flood during a torrential downpour. Surely a storm of that magnitude could sweep the messages off stones.

But I reject the graffiti idea. Instead I search for the highest, most worthy, of explanations for this primitive art. And in watching Rafe, my former student, deal with his students, I find the answer, or at least *an* answer, to the question: Why are these paintings here? This place could have been a classroom, I conclude, where young people were taught to communicate using symbols that were clearly abstractions. The landscape was their equivalent of our museums, zoos, libraries, that is, their source of mystery. It was here that students realized the world was not necessarily what they perceived it to be, that familiar shapes and textures could be arranged into an unfamiliar panorama, and where cacti stood like silent survivors who had made their uneasy peace with the nagging problem of wonder. And it was here that youth saw its elders, awed by the natural forms, respond by making pictures, then call the results "knowledge."

Aboriginal shamans were called *cusiya* or *guama,* depending on the region of the peninsula in which they lived. Pablo Martinez quotes the Dominican Luis Sales's description of these men:

> of extreme eloquence, indefatigable speech and singular efficacy in actions which is why they are held to be oracles. . . . Lies are believed with greater staunchness than if they were religious, thus [living] a life of indolence, these old men are given all food and favors and even though the Indians see the troops and missionaries beat the Shaman with whips, they still believe him.

In addition, the shamans "have knowledge of medicinal herbs." According to Martinez, that knowledge was not as commonly applied to wounds, however, as were tobacco juice, ligatures, or firebrands.

Evidently Cochimi math, like their medicine, functioned according to needs and expectations. Continues Martinez: "The arithmetic of the Californians was so elemental that the majority could hardly count to five. . . . When the counting entailed a large number, they expressed it by throwing fistfuls of earth into the air and blowing it to the sky." I can sympathize with that approach; I've felt like doing the same when confronted with twelve different measurements on two thousand parasitic worms. But the native method of handling large numbers also "led to confusion since they also expressed extraordinary delight by throwing earth into the air." Maybe the priests were just showing their ignorance of scientific research; most of my friends also express extraordinary delight with large numbers of data points.

Cochimi values show in their choices of food. They ate neither humans nor badgers; the footprints of badgers looked too much like those of humans. But they were not averse to hanging shells, lizards, or little mice from their pierced ears, nose, or lips. That behavior doesn't seem too strange to me; students at the University of Nebraska wear all sorts of stuff in their ears. The German missionary Jacob Baegert called the Indians "stupid, dull, stubborn, dirty, uncouth, ungrateful, lying, knavish, extremely lazy . . . disoriented, improvident, rash; a people who can never be tamed." Luis Sales agreed they were "loathsome, false and slovenly." Padre Juan de Ugarte was perhaps more insightful than the others: "Aborigines unexposed to missionaries gave water and treated us with utmost courtesy, while those who'd known priests for forty years didn't even have the respect to get up off the ground and respond to communication."

I get the sense, from reading Pablo Martinez, that regular psychic interactions with landscapes such as that north of Cataviña had a way of building a shield between humans and the forces that sought to domesticate them. In my experience such sacred places still function in that manner. Natural scenery associated with difficult, but deeply satisfying, intellectual endeavor reminds me of the positive feelings that come with tangible accomplishments, with personal discoveries. The river at Roscoe is thus a source of strength, of reaffirmation that I can and will be a naturalist, regardless of other demands.

Outside the rock overhang stands a *garambullo*. Memo, Pepe, Lupe, and Julio have carved their names on it; the scars have healed. Someone has taken a spray can to the mountain and produced a clover-shaped figure — a head — with two eye dots, one nose dot, and a mouth line curved very slightly downward. My sketch of this apparition stares out from the page with an unnerving vitality, the last far more a product of the artist's handiwork than of my rendition. Although it could have been intended as mockery of a bald-headed, big-eared acquaintance, the figure nevertheless communicates with me in an unexplained way. The spray-painted three-leaf clover man tells me it's all right to be amazed by the boulder fields north of Cataviña. After a climb up to the cave, I'm ready to believe that the ethereal quality of this obviously modern art is a product of the surrounding environment, or of a special sensitivity that was drawn to this hill by the patterns you could see from it. A nearby sign reads *no destruya las pinturas gracias*. Don't destroy the pictures, please. I should say not.

6

On the Beach

W e'll be in San Quintín in time to set up camp in the
daylight, Rafe promises, remembering another year
when he arrived after dark with a couple of dozen people
who had never slept out before. They tried to set up strange
tents in the Pacific wind that seemed to get colder by the
minute, then he had to make dinner for people who had
never used a gasoline stove and who wanted to do just one
thing: Get to the beach. They could hear the breakers off in
the night, the waves calling. But Rafe promises we'll be there
before dark this year. It doesn't happen; you never drive as
fast on Mexico 1 as your mind does on a map. Somewhere
south of town, along a blank stretch of highway, headlights
flash over a sign. I remember many such signs from southern
Oklahoma; usually they read "Jesus Saves" or "John 3:16" or
sometimes just "REPENT" in scrawled paint on rotten boards.
This one says "HONEYS RV CAMP." We turn in to "Honeys,"
following a narrow dirt road through sandy fields. Plastic and
paper blow across the trail like white birds scared into flight
by the wind.

Strange tents are still hard to set up in the dark. The ocean still calls. Flashlights stab through the wet black air. Real shorelines are the feel of salt, the sticky sand that stays in your clothes until weeks later, when they are put into a washer somewhere in the middle of the continent. There is no moon on this night; a stiff offshore wind blows; the crash of waves is followed quickly by water washing up over my feet. In the darkness I didn't realize I was so close to it. The fact that we can't see much seems to make the treasures we find all the more valuable. The students pick up everything: crab carapaces, sand dollars in various stages of disintegration, abraded bivalve shells in unmatched pairs. I walk toward two large shapes that appear at the end of my flashlight beam.

High up on the sand lie battered, narrow, wooden skiffs; scattered around them are freshly broken tests (skeletons, or "shells") of large purple sea urchins, the unmistakable sign of behavior as old as humanity: a wild harvest consumed on the spot. However cold the ocean in January, no matter what the techniques used to gather these few urchins, they must have been cracked and stripped of their ovaries as soon as the boat was dragged up above the tide line. The gonads were eaten fresh with only the grainy Pacific sand for flavoring. But it's a midwestern logic that constructs this scenario; in Baja California it might be worth the trip into town to sell the insides of a few grapefruit-sized sea urchins. The image of a fisherman raising the quivering tissues to his mouth is what I'm looking for, and finding, as a yellow beam plays over the worn boards of his boat and the debris scattered around its bow. I don't want to discover him putting a pound of gonads into a plastic bag, then walking to town for the few pesos sea urchin ovaries will bring. The latter image would violate the romantic vision that explorers are supposed to have of exotic lands.

In the morning Rafe begins his beach lessons with whatever has washed up on the sand: dead fish, a giant kelp strand with floats and holdfast still attached, and good shells — those not worn smooth or broken so badly that their unique features are destroyed. Like paleontologists, expert beach teachers can find particularly useful specimens in a seemingly disorganized jumble of items. Rafe likes the small shells. Glen is exceedingly picky; he's been to enough shorelines that he looks for additions to, not replicates of, the collection he already has back home. I prefer matched pairs — right and left values — especially ones with worm tubes or bryozoans; back in the city, shells with attached fauna are the most valuable as teaching material. Rafe gathers some sand dollars — *Dendraster excentricus* — then tells about seeing thousands of them on an underwater alluvial plain, all half buried in the sand, *on edge.* The image of sand dollars upright in long rows, like coins in slots, is so strange that he cannot hide his amusement. Even seasoned field men find some things so illogical, unexpected, irrational, that they just shrug when they tell their friends, then smile at themselves for acting like children.

Rafe holds out his discoveries and is immediately surrounded by a huddle of young heads. He talks about every piece in a manner developed from years of experience — what it is, what context it's embedded in, what it illustrates, and why this illustration is important. But the order in which he selects items is determined largely by luck; he doesn't, cannot, plan what we will encounter, beyond knowing that his teaching materials will have lived in the Pacific Ocean.

Rafe Payne on the beach reminds me of the mathematical phenomenon known as a "strange attractor." Certain equations, when solved over and over again, with each result put back into the equation in the next calculation, produce graphs whose shapes are highly predictable. Such regularity is a metaphor of our intents and methods in education. Inevitably, it seems, we search for ways to impose linearity on the system: high school counselors, career days, course numbers — 100, 200, 300, 400 — graduation, *job,* marriage, family, *promotion!* But the mathematicians tell us that hidden in these schemes is the potential for disaster. Change the value of a single constant, and the equation does not generate regularity at all but chaos.

In this unpredictable irregularity the theoreticians have uncovered a mysterious beauty. Their "constant" thus becomes a term that carries an enormous disruptive power. When deliberately applied to the equations, this power generates complexity that permeates the "system" from top to bottom, from the macroscopic to the microscopic properties. The beauty is that of repeated and intricate patterns, a *kind* of order emerging from apparent disorder, and significantly more elaborate, filled with much more information than the original line. In essence, for those processes that are applied time and again to the results of their own work, a single controlling factor often has the ability to change a straight line into a tree, unwavering predictability into a quivering, lively turbulence.

The powerful constant in this seaside equation south of San Quintín is the teacher's approach. Instead of a droning amplified monotone in a darkened auditorium at eight in the morning, we get seemingly casual talk mixed with the sounds of surf. Instead of a lesson plan, we get an unplanned lesson. On second thought, maybe the planning has occurred at a much higher level than I'm accustomed to, and thus is not so apparent as it might be in the city classroom. Rafe Payne has decided beforehand that the *sequence* of subjects is of little importance on a field trip, but the context within which each is studied is essential to his teaching. Thus instead of saying, "Today we study fish" and ignoring the kelp beside the dead fish, he picks up the kelp, then the fish, and talks about them both. And those who listen to his words and touch the specimens come away learning not about organisms per se, but about how to perceive nature. On the surface the intertidal sand appears disorganized, chaotic. But when a master teacher alters one constant — the standard approach — his equation produces an experience of profound beauty from a walk along the shore.

At one level the shoreline is fairly easy to express as a mathematical model. The dependent variables are crustacean parts, bivalve shells, strands of algae, echinoid tests, and a thousand other similar pieces of flotsam. These things occur in various proportions; that is, their numerical distributions are unequal. So are their sizes and weights. Their spatial arrangements are produced in part by a combination of wind, tides, and global weather and in part by evolutionary events — that is, the competing natural forces of anarchy and tradition, respectively. The abiotic factors are disruptive, the biological ones constraining. Both forces are highly creative, but the first recognizes few if any controls, while the second sees only a hint of freedom in the massive burden of its own history. And into this mess walks a man with a bunch of young people a long way from home.

The independent variable in our equation is a teacher who takes what the beach gives him and succeeds at his task by substituting for order an enormous breadth of knowledge, experience, and insight. By use of his skills he *causes* the natural world to serve as his classroom. But the beach provides something beyond the materials themselves, namely a freedom that can rarely be achieved inside buildings. These students expect order from a lab with numbered benches and chairs, and God help the instructor who tries to violate such expectations. On the beach they expect the unexpected. Rafe cannot help, then, but teach by example; we'll forget the scientific name of the Pismo clam, but we won't forget Rafe holding its shell in his hand and telling us what to look for. The notebooks are filled with sketches and facts; the heads are filled with awe; and the memories contain a role model — one who studies nature seriously, without excuses, simply out of love and curiosity.

He picks up a dried fish head and talks about it for fifteen minutes. By the time he finishes, the crowd around him knows a little more than it did before about fish, and a lot more than it did about what to do if you're suddenly confronted with a stiff and stinking assemblage of hard bone, curling scales, vacant eye sockets, and gaping mouth. A few small sharks, dripping slime, lying in a tub beside a panga, are examined with loving care. We get a lecture on teeth, gill openings, heterocercal tails. Kelp pieces litter the sand. Rafe chooses one with a fine fur of hydrozoan polyps. We hear about colonial growth form, planula larvae, and the possible evolutionary origin of bilaterally symmetrical animals. He waits until he finds a whole individual of *Macrocystis* before he untangles it from the debris and talks about kelp, its many commercial uses, biologists' efforts to farm it.

I try to imagine what my class of 270 eighteen-year-old freshmen would do, back in a lecture hall in Lincoln, Nebraska, with such a random array of topics. In the past thirty years I've encountered nearly ten thousand students, from preschoolers to retired people, and they have all responded most enthusiastically to opportunities for pure exploration. The difference between an organized lesson and a field trip is in the students' minds. They *know* the freshman lab is a well-worn exercise that can usually be done in three hours and that the lecture has been repeated so often it's dogma. But in the field they ignore the fact that somebody has already described most of the organisms they see. In school, life is brought to them; in the field, they must go seek it. So when I ask: Which is more like their future — the lab, the book, or the beach? — the answer is obvious.

A number of washed-up items reveal interactions among members of the continental shelf community. Few molluscan shells last for very long without acquiring bryozoans, sponges, barnacles, and polychaete tubes. Within an hour Rafe picks up two almost identical, palm-sized shells of the Pismo clam, a species of *Tivela*. They are both right valves and thus from different individuals. One is clean; on the inside surface, muscle and pallial line scars stand out as clearly as in a textbook diagram; on the outside, an intact calcareous layer and thin periostracum retain their field guide colors and brownish bands. The other shell is encrusted with, and bored into by, numerous other organisms.

If I had to choose one of these two shells to keep, it would be the second, upon which tiny white coils reveal the presence of serpulids, sedentary polychaetes distantly related to earthworms, but with their anterior ends modified into a brushlike fan of tentacles used to strain food particles out of the sea. The word "serpulid" is derived from the family name Serpulidae, which in turn applies to a family of annelids that secrete tubes made of calcium salts. The shape of their tubes is almost diagnostic; the tubes of many California and Mexican Pacific species are small, coiled into a tight, slightly imperfect spiral affixed to various substrates, including kelp, rocks, and shells. Among twenty or thirty serpulids on this single clam valve, I see genetically determined behavioral traits: The shape and composition of their tubes allows me to distinguish them from other polychaete families. Variation among individual worms is equally as obvious: The tubes are not all exactly the same shape, and their microscopic surface architecture differs slightly between specimens, within the species' limits. They vary also in size, revealing a history of colonization. I also see dumb luck: The motile larvae that landed on this dead clam were fortunate; the ones that settled on live sea urchins probably got snipped in half by tiny beak-like pincers called pedicellaria.

Through the hand lens, part of the shell appears to be covered by a microscopic mosaic pavement, a colony of bry-ozoans that has spread by multiplication of genetically identical parts across the inside of the shell; the blocks are the individuals, called zooids. Bryozoans are ancient, highly colonial, filter-feeding animals that strain food particles from the water by means of ciliated tentacles. Individuals may vary in shape according to their position in the colony; the first occupants can be distinguished from their progeny. That is always the case with pioneers, I remember. The growing edge, the youngest zooids, are slightly different in form from the older masses behind them. The young are thrust out at the borders of society with only their history for guidance. Beneath a powerful microscope this colony would reveal its intricacies — cells in which the members spend their lives, internal partitions by which they're separated from neighbors, the lids they use to cover their only port to the outside world, and the lashing filaments on those lids, whips functioning to keep the colony free of swimming, searching larvae, as the bryozoan crust itself once was.

Bryozoan fossils occur in rocks that are four hundred million years old. In these fossils one sees evidence for the same kinds of changes that living species go through during colony development. The founders can be determined, as can the sequence by which an individual became an adult, the role one zooid must have played in the group, and the characteristic shape of the species' colony — flat, spiraled, or branching like a bush. Thus the clam shell in my hand could be an Ordovician fossil, and I would still be able to "see" the life of a bryozoan species on it as clearly as I'm able to decipher the record on a shell collected today from the beach at San Quintín. The colonized shell is far more of a treasure than the clean one. The numerous other animals on it provide complexity, a feature of all communities, and their positions hint at interactions. Individual sizes and colony shapes suggest unique histories, another common property of living organisms. This tangible evidence of imagined events all make the specimen encrusted with worm tubes, barnacles, and bryozoans of inestimable value. Far from San Quintín in space and time, the old shell can be used to generalize principles of life for students who may never have been to a beach. They can touch the specimen, look at it through a hand lens, and draw its picture in their notebooks, even as I'm doing, standing on the wet sand, ignoring for the moment the rest of the Pacific Ocean and its inhabitants. And when I ask what they've learned, they'll tell me that individuals have just one chance to find a suitable clam shell upon which to spend their lives, and there's every reason to believe they will then have to share the space. And neither I nor these future students will need to explain the analogy to one another.

Down the beach, having wandered, watching, then stopping, and now turning some stinking discoveries over and over in his hands, again surrounded by the huddle of young American heads, Rafe uses his words to give whatever he has found the same properties as the colonized Pismo valve. His explanations reveal complexity, interaction, and history in a crab leg, a gull wing, or a clump of pickleweed. Thus a master teacher shows his students what to look *for* rather than what to look *at*. By this means he converts his followers into searchers. As neophytes, they have walked past many important bits and pieces, not knowing their value, and have chosen keepsakes for their beauty or strangeness, rather like a wealthy art collector making his way through galleries hung with unknown painters. But with Rafe's eyes to guide them, they've started to see history and process in every shell, carapace, or bone. "What is it?" evolves into "How did it get here in this condition?" — a question that marks the beginning of a transition from tourist seeking diversion to scientist haunted by curiosity.

How effective is this form of teaching? Later in the afternoon of the day of Rafe's first beach walk, I get a chance to observe the results of his morning's session. South of San Quintín lies El Rosario, where the highway turns inland along the south rim of the arroyo of the Río del Rosario, and where we will stop, several miles from the ocean, to look at sea urchins again. Here tens of thousands of tests are heaped in mounds that in places are shoulder high. In the glaring sun I shield my eyes and note that some piles are still purple — they must have been left recently — and others are bleached white. When you crack an urchin's shell, the animal is as good as dead; it cannot repair the damage. Standing in the El Rosario dump, now just as much a classroom as the beach was earlier, Rafe explains what parts are actually used: The gonads are stripped out, bagged in plastic, and sent to Japan. Americans don't eat urchin ovaries in sushi parlors, but the Japanese do.

Then I remember the beach at night and my earlier assessment of Mexican economics. If I interpreted the physical evidence correctly, a day's work for one fisherman was half a dozen *Strongylocentrotus franciscanus*. How can there be enough protein in sea urchin gonads to make it worth anyone's efforts to collect them? But I live in a land where meat is bought and sold in semitrailer loads, not in ounces gathered from cold salt water. There has never been a time in my life in the United States when I could not go to a store, usually within a few blocks of where I lived, and buy as much beef, pork, chicken, and lamb as I had money or wishes to buy. Nor are my companions much different from me in this respect. Shown the piles of broken shells, they ignore the sociological implications of this massive harvest and immediately begin poking through the skeletons for urchin "teeth."

Sea urchins have a beautifully complex set of bonelike "ossicles" associated with their mouth, which is located on the bottom surface. This latter, seemingly trivial, observation has caught many an introductory biology student unprepared when asked about anatomical features that define the various body regions of sea stars, sea cucumbers, and all their relatives. In the sea urchin, characteristically shaped skeletal plates known as ambulacral ossicles, rows of tube feet, and spines of particular design all converge on the mouth. But inside the animal, surrounding the pharynx, are the teeth, known collectively as "Aristotle's lantern." I look over the piles of urchin tests, breathing in the reek of dead sea animals. Inside every shell is a perfect lantern. The students climb on the mounds, feet sinking into the mess, every crunching step sending up a cloud of sickly sweet rot odor. They pick through the skeletons; each comes up with a handful of Aristotle's lanterns. In their past, no doubt, they have been asked to dissect out the urchin teeth, a classical exercise in invertebrate zoology. But time and decay accomplish what scalpels and fine scissors cannot always do: the removal of Aristotle's lantern intact, perfectly preserved, bleached, an only slightly smelly souvenir.

Back home I have a supply of these specimens left over from past undergraduate labs, most of them cut out by young people working hard to get into medical school. I wonder how many hands have discovered themselves suited for delicate surgery as a result of this dissection exercise. The opportunity to become a physician may open to some of these young people later; but for the moment, I conclude, Rafe's sense of what is important in the world has been successfully transferred. Surrounded by dead and rotten animal remains, rusted cans, empty oil containers, broken furniture, padding, springs, strips of tire rubber, shattered jars and bottles, they ignore it all and search for the largest, cleanest, and best-preserved specimens of Aristotle's lantern.

7

Keeper of the Keys

$\bigcirc$ nce upon a time, when searching for a symbol to represent the conservation movement, I selected the marsh
wren because it complains loudly and repeatedly whenever
an intruder enters its domain, displaying the audacity typical
of idealists who envision themselves as saviors. When I made
this choice, I was standing in a place called Keystone Marsh,
so I called the marsh wren the "keeper of the keys" and
imagined having to ask its permission in order to enter the
cattails. Keystone Marsh became a model for all natural areas,
and its avian proprietor came to represent an internal constraint on our willingness to alter an environment without
truly understanding, or even considering, the consequences.

My analysis of this symbolism was eventually published in
a book called *Keith County Journal,* in which it was read by a
young man named Wiley Roberson. Wiley had his own "Keith
County," namely Bahía de los Ángeles, and he chose his own
keeper of the keys — that element of nature claiming possession of and responsibility for Bahía and its surrounding landscape. To him, Mexico's Bay of Angels was a sacred place. I
hesitate to say he believed it to be occupied by spirits, but he

was at least willing to assign roles to various nonhuman entities in the maintenance of that gestalt essential to the Baja
California mystique. Wiley met me at the Los Angeles (California) airport. Rafe introduced us, and Wiley got right to the
point.

"After your first trip to Baja," he said, "come back and tell
me who you think is the 'keeper of the keys' to Bahía." From
the look on his face, I knew he had thought long and hard
about this matter and that his thoughts had been stimulated
by his encounter with both the spirit and its physical form.
Something, possibly a plant or an animal or even a nonbio-
logical phenomenon, always reminded Wiley to walk gently
and carefully in Baja California. But none of the species I
expected to see matched my reading of this young man — a
person who had responded, both intellectually and emotionally, not only to the Mexican landscape but also to Rafe's
teaching. I couldn't see how a quintessentially lazy pelican or
a brutally self-serving gull could represent Wiley's sense of
responsibility.

"Sure." I accepted the challenge, knowing that in the search
for an answer, I'd sort through the entire spectrum of personal metaphors derived from deep-seated views of the natural world. The symbol would be, above all, unique. Vision is
not independent of history, either at the individual or the
social level. In this sense we each generate our own reality by
observing it, an experience so well known to the particle
physicists as to be one of their fundamental precepts.

So I awake in the darkness to the gulls' warning that the
sun, still well hidden behind Isla Cabeza de Caballo, will
nevertheless rise, and on my first morning at Bahía de los
Ángeles I begin to think about the assignment. A cold wind
washes down from the mountains, swirls around the cabin
corner, and shakes my canvas cot, whose legs rest unevenly
on the patio's granite slabs. A falling tide surges gently through

the boulders at my feet. I am in a strange and foreign place — another person's intellectual haven. The plants and animals here have not yet affected my life, at least not directly, but they have had a powerful impact on the thoughts of other biologists. And as the darkness turns to gray over the islands, I suddenly realize the significance of Wiley's request: A student has become teacher, a seemingly simple task has evolved into a personal learning device, and a brief exchange of words in an airport has set me off on a voyage of discovery throughout that vast wilderness built of symbols.

Behind Horsehead Island the sky turns to red, then red-orange; the color is reflected in the bay. Heavy wings flap in the chill air; a flurry of protest reveals a prize scrap of tissue found, or captured, then stolen, maybe several times, before finally being consumed. A thousand times in the next weeks, and on subsequent trips, I'll see the Heermann's gulls exhibit their all-consuming inner drive: thievery. Dark immatures sit, sometimes patiently, it seems, around a handsome adult, who in turn watches the intertidal rocks, the fishing boats, red bill pointing this way and that, eyes checking every pelican, every human, each panga, waiting, poised but waiting, for another to find something — *any*thing — to eat.

The red glow and reflections quickly fade to yellow; this vermilion sea is, above all, ephemeral. Gull traffic picks up; time to get out on the street, heist a broken oyster, grab a little shred of ray skin from your partner instead of getting your own, even though the dead ray lies at your feet. Heermann's gull is endemic to the Sea of Cortés, and in contrast to most other gull species, which tend to be opportunistic feeders — grabbing whatever they can regardless of how it becomes available — Heermann's exists almost solely by, and seemingly for the joy of, taking food first obtained by others.

Once, sitting on the sand at Bahía Concepción, I saw a young Heermann's sprinting toward the dark cliffs, carrying a small octopus. The quickness with which its companions responded, the viciousness, determination, and acrobatics of the subsequent chase, all made me rethink my impression of avian mental capacities. They *knew* the young gull had picked up a supreme delicacy. I had thought that they could get excited about anything, so long as it was stolen. But this event told me they could, in unmeasurable fractions of a second, distinguish a really great tidbit, like an octopus, from a so-so snack, such as a shark eye. A sanctuary manager is not supposed to be a greedy, self-serving thief who fends for himself only when presented with the most wonderful of rewards. Heermann's gull may be a fixture in the Gulf of California, but it's not a keeper of anyplace.

Down the beach, toward Guillermo's cantina, I hear voices. The sound of foreign tongues always makes me wish I had been raised in a multilingual household. Years earlier the marsh wren's vocalizations had drawn my attention and had led me to give it imagined traits. So now, having eliminated Heermann's gull as a possible keeper of the keys, I sort through the natural noise and try to analyze the sounds that break the morning stillness. Looking out over the shoreline I discover a bird that brings to mind one of the strangest biological events that has ever happened to me: A double-crested cormorant fell out of the sky over Norman, Oklahoma. I picked up the bird and painted its picture. That's the whole story, but I remember it whenever I see a cormorant, which is fairly often.

At the Bay of Angels, cormorants stand silently in the early morning on the algae-covered darkened granite, turning their heads, black birds making black silhouettes, spreading their wings slightly. My imagination turns cormorants into stoic philosophers, laboring to get airborne, sinking into the water at the approach of lesser intellects, studying, always studying, their environment: What does it mean to be a rock?

In how many forms does the ripple exist? How can a pelican be so stupid and still survive? Why fly? The cormorant asks: Are cacti reincarnations of fish? Is stone alive? Is there a God and does He look like a cormorant? Do barnacles serve a purpose? And so his life is filled with unanswered — and unanswerable — questions. The cormorant is not the symbolic proprietor of Bahía; he says nothing, expresses no moral outrage, makes no emotional response whatsoever to my presence; he has no insight into my intents, only curiosity about my deeper essence. He pulls in his wings, turns his back to me, his chest to the rising sun. Why do people watch birds? He poses a rhetorical question. The cormorant on the next rock turns her bill toward the first. Why do birds watch people? she responds, just as rhetorically. And together they sit, pondering their rhetorical questions silently.

A pair of oystercatchers appears, stepping among the small boulders, focused on the minutiae between their feet, their red chisel bills making accent marks on the dark, wet stone surfaces around them. No; there are not enough oystercatchers to claim Bahía, and besides, they are too occupied with their own immediate concerns. Far out over the bay, beyond the old launch tethered to its buoy, the boobies come to work. They press the air with pointed wings, cruising, ignoring all but their meal flashing silver beneath them through the cold, shadowed sea behind an island. They plunge, strike the water at full hurtling speed, then surface flying, crossing the air-water interface almost as quickly as when they dive. The boobies are creatures of extreme beauty, easily recognized as superb evidence for the Grand Design — the idea that earth was made, down to the finest detail, by a Supreme Being. How else could animals be so perfectly suited to the lives they lead? Or so the logic goes. But *Sula nebouxii* could never be the one responsible for a bay. Although its dive and flight are reasons enough why Bahía, and all places like it, must be preserved, the boobie does not have the character of a keeper; artists are expensive but necessary elements of a civilized community, but you never try to turn them into watchdogs or chief executive officers.

Thus my search goes on. The cold wind that has spent the last several dark hours persistently searching for every tiny gap between my sleeping bag and ears dies down slightly. I expand my list of candidates for the role of proprietor, trying to remember all the possibilities, from birds to invertebrates. An hour later, still in this pensive state, coffee in hand, I wander down to the beach and start poking through the sand and shells.

At the upper, high-tide edge of the boulder field, *Nerita funiculata* clings to the rocks. This most common of snails is the signature of the Bahía intertidal. But is it the keeper? *Nerita funiculata* does not strike me as being the kind of animal that would capture Wiley Roberson's fancy, and to me it seems more a fine species upon which to do research than a symbol of human values. It fulfills all the criteria for the subject of a master's thesis: numerous, present in a wide range of sizes (ages), evidently adapted to a life of daily transition from salt water to air (one of the most osmotically stressful environments available to living organisms) and finally, a member of a group of species related taxonomically (the other nerites) and ecologically (the other intertidal snail species). Thus a physiological ecologist might ask questions about functional differences between related species occupying different microenvironments. Presumably such questions would focus on the problems of evolutionary divergence within a family of snails sharing common ancestry. Alternatively, one could study the way in which unrelated forms have colonized similar habitats.

By "microenvironment" and "habitat" I mean a rather restricted combination of light, temperature, moisture, associated species, and physical structure of rocks and sand. The upper part of the intertidal zone is exposed to air for a much longer period than the lower. There exists a gradient of potential physiological stress as well as a progression of different situations in which organisms must find food and reproduce, from lower intertidal to upper. A human who walks out of the water, having explored the shallows offshore with snorkel and fins, thus steps across a series of boundaries established by various species' genetically endowed traits. As the tide falls, I make a catalog of these species: the various crabs that for good reason spend the dry and daylight hours beneath a stone, the snails — *Nerita funiculata,* of course, but also *Tegula* and *Turbo.* I pick a handful for closer study, comparing their ornamentation, sizes, and shapes of apertures, then smiling with the realization that most are not "snails" at all but ghost shells. As I peer into the aperture of a perfect *Tegula felipensis,* a small cluster of red legs appears. Slowly the imagery I'm searching for reaches out of all the shells, tentatively at first, then more boldly. Regardless of what species Wiley Roberson has chosen, I have found my keeper of the keys, the one responsible for Bahía de los Ángeles. It is a hermit crab named *Clibanarius digueti.*

Hermit crabs are among the most wondrous, yet common, members of the intertidal and continental shelf communities. Crabs in general hide; they shy away from passing shadows, back into crevices or under rocks and, depending on the species, twiddle their eyes in almost iconographic alertness. Species that stand their ground earn names inspired by severely pinched fingers, such as *Callinectes bellicosus,* but the vast majority behave as if they know they would make a delicious meal. Mole crabs dig burrows. Members of the genus *Pinnixia* get sealed inside leathery worm tubes. And other species become locked forever inside sponges and corals. At one time an ancestral hermit crab, an ancestral *cangrejo ermitaño,* must have backed into an empty shell when threatened. Since that time its descendants have refined shell selection into a natural art form — a combination of ballet and fight, a behavior that accomplishes something obvious only in retrospect, and then only to humans: the creation of a sort of "snail heaven" in which the gastropod spirit lives on after the mollusc itself is gone.

Clibanarius digueti is a small species, inhabiting shells from the size of *Nassarius,* only a few millimeters long, up to *Turbo* and *Tegula,* which are maybe an inch across at the widest point. *C. digueti*'s legs are a strange semigloss red and are covered with light bluish spots. On its back, dark streaks begin at the anterior end of the carapace, then branch toward the lateral and posterior edges of the dorsal exoskeleton. In the lab at the Vermilion Sea Field Station, I study one specimen, adjusting and focusing the microscope, carefully drawing the lines, dots, hairs, and bristles. Naturalists always seem to start with structure; we must know exactly how something is built before we can talk about its other properties. But drawing a picture of an animal reminds me that biologists can never avoid the evidence for genetic control of pattern formation or the question whether, or how, the environment has influenced the process. Pencil in hand, I must decide now whether the markings on the left and right side of a crab's back are perfect mirror images of each other. They are not. My keeper has inherited the genes to make two sets of branching lines, but the cytoplasm in which those genes lay buried dictated the finer details.

In a dish of sea water, beneath the microscope, one *C. digueti* emerges from its shell. I switch lenses, zooming in on the antennule — appendages that look like thin, downward-curved blades, with a fringe of stiff long bristles, on stalks extending forward between the eyes. The antennule tips are in constant motion. These structures are sensory; *C. digueti* is "tasting" its environment constantly with extraordinarily delicate and fragile organs held out front into the ocean. The antennule tips are essential for survival, but they are highly vulnerable to injury. They remind me of ideals, or values, held out, vibrating, assessing the intellectual climate in which they are bathed.

Something about the movement of the legs catches my eye. I wet my hand, then hold the shell in it. Again, slowly, the crab emerges, then crawls up my palm and out to the tip of my finger. Through the hand lens I can see it touching my skin over and over again, disconcertingly purposefully — right leg one, placed here, there, four or five places; then right leg two, then left, each in turn exploring the crevices of my fingerprints as carefully as it would investigate a potential new shell. I imagine I can feel the tiny leg tips, knowing that the feeling might be only in my mind because I'm so large compared to my companion. The touching pattern is repeated. What is this? the crab is "asking." The leg movements seem vaguely familiar; they mimic those of a planetary lander. Surely the human fingertip must be as strange to *Clibanarius digueti* as the surface of Mars is to us. Are we as suspicious of Mars as *C. digueti* seems to be of me? I prefer to think not. We have little to fear from Mars.

Numerous published reports suggest that hermit crab populations are limited by the supply of available homes. One kind of crab may use the shells of all the local gastropods and may inhabit shells much larger than required for the weight of the species. For example, species of *Clibanarius* have been shown to use shells up to twelve times their body weight, even though a one-to-four crab:shell ratio is optimal for egg production. Although the average clutch size for *C. digueti* at Bahía de los Ángeles has not been determined, in other members of the genus it ranges from about 200 to over 7,500 eggs. In a number of hermit species, clutch size is a function of shell size: The smaller the shell, the fewer the eggs. The crab beneath my microscope is a reflection of those factors that govern the life and death of *snails* in the Bahía intertidal. So my candidate keeper is tied inextricably to an entire ecosystem, which in turn has a set of integral and necessary properties that cannot be separated from one another.

Of all the intertidal crabs, only hermits appear to seek the sun's warmth, gathering on the tops of barnacle-covered granite rocks. I can tell these shells are occupied by something other than snails: At my touch *C. digueti* draws up into its shell, which then rests lightly on the boulder surface; snails clamp firmly to the wet stone with their muscular, mucus-covered feet. Live snails also respond to environmental conditions in a rather species-specific manner: *Nerita funiculata* alone covers the upper rock surfaces when the tide falls in the shadowy afternoon; in the darkness later, the *Nerita* are gone, have crawled down into the sand, but the limpet *Collisella stanfordiana* has taken *Nerita*'s place.

Both tides and daylight are cyclic, almost wave-form, physical events. If we plotted the water's distance from any fixed point on shore against time, the resultant graph would look like a wavy line of certain amplitude and frequency. If we did the same with the amount of light — night and day — the results would be similar. But light cycles are produced by the turning of the earth on its axis, while tides are caused by interactions between the earth and its moon, and these two cosmic processes are not on exactly the same schedule. For this reason, some low tides occur in the darkness and others in the daylight.

The shell populations that cover the shoreline boulders vary with different combinations of time and tide. If the tide begins to fall in late afternoon, nerites and limpets remain on, or migrate to, the upper rock surfaces. When the tide starts to drop in the morning, the nerites move down between the boulders, the limpets remain below water, and the only shells on top, in the sun and air, are those containing hermit crabs. The intertidal mollusc and hermit crab communities are thus given temporary structure by cyclic physical processes. The "vibrations" produced by the rising and setting of the sun and the orbiting of the moon are very slow compared to those of electrons. Yet they are vibrations nevertheless, and in a manner analogous to the famous quantum mechanics experiments with subatomic particle beams, light and tide produce a distinctive pattern in which the occupation of rock tops occurs, or does not, depending on the summing or canceling of waves generated by celestial bodies.

One popular translation of quantum theory is the assertion that reality is created by the observer. I accept this idea; my assignment of the role of keeper to *C. digueti* generates ideas, concepts, expressions of value, that are all capable of being transmitted from one human to another. Quantum theorists also contend that position and momentum cannot be simultaneously determined with great accuracy. This rule is certainly applicable to the Bahía intertidal zone; simply by watching the invertebrate community over a single day/night/tide cycle, I can see the transitory nature of any one particular arrangement of parts. Conversely, by describing in detail a single instantaneous structure, I lose the sense of change; my photograph taken at 1/500 of a second captures position but shows no movement. And so my vision of this assemblage of animals, with its emphasis on mollusc shells that may or may not be occupied by molluscs, extends from the shores of Bahía de los Ángeles down into the mostly vacant depths of atoms and up into the largely empty reaches of the solar system.

Would this vision have formed had Wiley Roberson not given me an assignment, and had *Clibanarus digueti* not taken on the role of keeper? I don't know. What I do know is that the concept — that of a wild creature exhibiting traits analogous to those of a proprietor — is infective. One night at the Vermilion Sea Field Station we were having a discussion around the fire. Rafe brought up the wren chapter of *Keith County Journal.* I mentioned the meeting with Wiley, then revealed my choice of a keeper of Bahía, explaining what I had been doing for the past several days and nights down on my knees among the intertidal boulders, namely studying crabs. It is a tradition among classes who visit VSFS to paint a mural inside the building to commemorate their trip. A few days after our fireside seminar, the students painted a picture of *C. digueti* on the wall of the Vermilion Sea Field Station. In its chelae the crab was holding a ring of keys.

On a sunny morning at low tide, the rock tops are covered with a mixture of species' shells, a sure giveaway that *C. digueti* are in them instead of their original owners. Diversity is thus on display. This boulder-surface parade reveals that the environment contains many more kinds of organisms than a human would ordinarily see at first glance. And it is this element of the keeper-analogy story that led me to choose *C. digueti* over any of the other potential symbols. The tiny hermit crab works continuously, in a manner essential to its own existence, to save the shells, and in so doing it preserves variety, then shows the world the results of its labor. *Nassarius tiarula, Acanthina angelica, Turbo fluctuosus, Tegula felipensis, Nerita funiculata, Columbella fuscata, Olivella, Liocerthium,* and *Crassispira* species — *C. digueti* occupies them all, and probably many more, I'd discover, if only there were more time to search. I look at the rocks in the morning and say: There are a dozen kinds of snails here that I didn't see at first, and I would not have seen them now except for the behavior of *Clibanarius digueti.* The world is not as simple as I thought it was.

This observation also reminds me of another experience,

loosely connected to the world of pop quantum mechanics, that shaped my entire teaching philosophy. I gave a strange writing assignment to a class of a hundred honors students. The raw material to support this task was a centerfold picture from a large-format wildlife calendar — a great egret, *Egretta alba,* flying low over relatively still water. The photographer had captured the great white bird against a dark blue background, as well as its reflection, also white on blue, but of course somewhat distorted by the interplay of small ripples, light, water, and lenses. The assignment was to describe this picture, but there were some rules: (1) money, politics, the military, agriculture, health, sex, sports, or religion could not be mentioned; (2) depending on the initial of the student's last name, the student had to write as if he or she lived in a world that:

a. contained an unlimited supply of fossil fuel (A–E);
b. began in 1965 (F–J);
c. was one of millions, maybe billions, of identical worlds throughout the universe (K–O);
d. was completely unique, i.e., life did not exist anywhere else in the universe (P–S); or
e. consisted only of all that can be seen or touched and nothing else (T–Z); and

(3) the paper had to be three pages of double-spaced typing.

The problem was not unlike the Bahía keeper one — difficult, with a solution that was both highly constrained and not unique, a rigidly defined task that could be accomplished in a thousand ways, each involving the generation of reality by an observer. Both assignments illustrate what I call the creative paradox, namely the liberating effects of extreme constraints. In response to my prohibiting any mention of money, politics, the military, agriculture, health, sex, sports, or religion, one student began his exercise with the words "you have taken away all that is dearest to me," then proceeded to write a magnificent discourse on a world that is only one of billions of identical ones throughout the universe. Awakening on the Vermilion Sea Field Station patio that first morning, I realized I had boarded the plane in order to get away from all that was dearest to that student, an act that ultimately left me alone with shells and crabs and gulls and cormorants and a nagging request from Wiley Roberson.

The heron example is only one out of dozens that I could have chosen from my last decade of experiences in teaching. In each case, simply by trying to remove every influence of the media or of the stereotypical "important things," we come to see ourselves as a natural part of the universe rather than masters of it. I imagine what the responses might be to a future assignment in which the subject is a hermit crab instead of an egret. In three pages, tell your parents why you have dropped out of medical school in order to study *Clibanarius digueti* for the rest of your life. ("Dear Mom and Dad, When I came to college you told me don't smoke, don't wear short skirts, don't pick my nose, don't date weirdos, and don't embarrass the family. Well, unfortunately, I'm about to do the latter. You see, there's this species of hermit crab . . .") Answer the criticism of the university's installation of your forty-foot-high bronze hermit crab sculpture on the library mall. (DO OVER. Todd, your claim that "at least it's not as abstract as the one that's there now" really doesn't address the assignment.) Design a museum gallery that explains how *C. digueti* illustrates the concept of ecological interdependency. (" + Well done, Tami; I like your idea of a ten-foot-high *Tegula* shell that kids can walk into and thus share with an appropriately scaled-up hermit crab. Have you considered a set of kid-sized shells that they could play musical chairs

with in order to illustrate the concept of limited natural resources?") Guess who's my "keeper of the keys"? (Okay,
Wiley, I'll give it a try.)

Later, driving along a dark road beside the ocean, Rafe and I
fall to talking about Wiley Roberson. Rafe tells me which
natural phenomenon Wiley considered the proprietor of Bahía
de los Ángeles: the wind — the blistering hot summer wind
that takes all water and will to work right out of your insides,
the unpredictable wind that makes you run for shore, the
cold winter wind that comes inside your sleeping bag and
bites and reminds you that you sleep softly at his mercy. Yes,
I can see that; I can see how Wiley would look to the forces
that dictated what he could and could not do. He would not
be satisfied with only responsibility; he would want his keeper
to have power, real power, not just words and ideas and examples.

The one dim headlight of an old pickup truck, coming
toward us, reveals the sleeping faces behind me. They are
young and impressionable, a long way from home, and not
accustomed to people who think the planet belongs to animals and winds. So I think, with a little bit of luck, sometime
in the future, each of them will encounter a stranger in an
airport, a person who sends them on a mission of discovery
to find their own symbol of which part of nature is responsible for the bay or forest or desert or grassland into which
they have chosen to set foot.

8

Rock Pelicans

The Vermilion Sea Field Station patio is a magnificent place upon which to sit and contemplate the busy parade that characterizes rich subtropical coastal waters. Cormorants labor through the wind toward glistening intertidal rocks. Gulls in various stages of maturity sleep or squabble, then dash for an inbound panga. Mergansers push through the shallows, their heads underwater, looking for small fish. Brown and blue-footed boobies plunge out of the sky and into the bay. A reddish egret glides in from the north, landing on the largest boulder out beyond the low-tide line. Oystercatchers move deliberately in and out of the barnacle-covered granite blocks. A frigate bird hangs over the distant guano-iced and twisted stone islands. Porpoises arc through the mirage line between the far-off broken lava and the glassy surface of the bay. Sea lions poke their whiskered snouts into the air, turn, then dive. The bountiful show of Bahía is in stark contrast to the dismembered technology of the Ocañas' auto repair shop on the other side of the field station. But one member of this natural theater company looks as if it's been built from the multifarious Ford Motor Company parts lying scattered in the sand on the landward side of VSFS: the brown pelican.

Few acts are more foreign to the average citizen than studying a single wild animal for extended periods of time. Indeed, such lack of focus might define "average citizen," were it not for the constraint that in biology, the labeling of organisms must be based on traits they possess rather than on ones they are missing. Who in his or her right mind would watch a single sparrow for twelve hours running, or a single beetle, or one butterfly, or even one pelican for thirty minutes? But people in my business consider it a privilege to study an individual animal's behavior for hours, even months and years. Some think that one of these days the opportunity may be gone. So, far away from home, with no authority to answer to, I wallow in the luxury of watching one ugly, ungainly, seemingly misdesigned animal, namely, a specimen of *Pelicanus occidentalis,* twenty yards from the patio edge.

The brown pelican is a combination of contradictions with little obvious correspondence between form and function. For example, the familiar throat pouch seems ideally suited for carrying fish, but regardless of what the classic limerick says ("His beak holds more than his belly can"), pelicans generally don't carry food in their pouches. In fact, neither the origin nor the function of this most distinctive characteristic is really clear, either to the casual observer or to the careful one. I don't want to believe that the throat pouch is large just because the pelican's bill is long, so I keep looking for something in the bird's behavior that would suggest a function to match the structure. If we let our imagination run wild, all sorts of possible uses come to mind, for example, temperature regulation (through the dissipation of body heat), aggressive displays, or courtship. Theoretically, experiments could be done to "prove" the role of the pouch in pelican life. But these studies might be of more interest as intellectual exercises than as real biology. That is, we might gain more insight into pelican biology by trying to design the experiments than by actually doing them.

Pelicans are related to frigate birds, cormorants, and boobies, and all possess certain features, including a hind toe turned inward and forward, webbing that connects all four toes, a wishbone fused to the sternum, eleven primary feathers, a tufted oil gland, and, of course, a throat pouch. The frigate bird inflates its pouch into a red balloon as part of the mating ritual. But the pelican, with a much larger pouch, does not inflate it, although the skin becomes red during courtship, fading once eggs are laid. On the other hand, the pelicaniform pouch has another possible function, namely, to hold vomit, since these animals feed their young by regurgitation. In fact, the pouch looks as if it were designed for that purpose. But newly hatched pelicans are so weak and helpless that they can't even raise their heads. The mother has to spit up and let the juices run down into the baby's mouth. Even when the nestlings get larger, they don't eat vomit right out of the pouch. Instead, they poke their heads all the way down into the parent's gullet.

In my hour of watching a single pelican, I see nothing that hints at the function of the pouch. I see an enormous amount of snoozing, a little bit of preening, some defecation, and a casual flight over to the rock jetty near Guillermo's. There the bird joins a group that radiates unconcern, heads settling slowly back between their wings. The pouch gets stretched once in a while, apparently by virtue of its being attached to the bill, which is waved about simply because it is connected to the head; but the pouch never gets *used*. I see nothing to suggest that this structure is necessary to a pelican's survival.

Far away, out over Bahía de los Ángeles, a pelican dives, folding its wings back at the last second, slipping easily if not delicately into the silver blue waves, then surfacing, trails of water gushing out the sides of its bill, and finally gulping and stretching, choking down something I can't identify through the spotting scope. If the pouch functions as a fishnet, that use is exceedingly brief and hidden from view. The bird sits high on the water for a few seconds before clambering laboriously into the air, a medium within which awkwardness is miraculously transformed into extreme grace. Why, I wonder, has the general public, through popular literature, art, and film, focused on the pouch instead of the wing as the bird's most distinctive trait? What makes us tend to pick out the most bizarre feature, rather than the most elegant one, to sustain our mental image of the pelican?

Scholars, or their equivalents, have always noted the structural features that seem to "best" characterize animals. Cro-Magnon cave paintings of bison and mammoths are anatomically correct as well as artistically elegant. During the fourth century B.C. Aristotle followed the same tradition in his *Historia animalium* (ten volumes), *De partibus animalium* (four volumes), and *De generatione animalium* (five volumes). Aristotle made mistakes, however, most notably in cases where he accepted others' observations of animals he had never seen. Herodotus, for example, claimed that a crocodile's lower jaw was fixed, while the upper one was hinged to the skull, and Aristotle repeated the error, which he would likely have discovered immediately had he ever studied a specimen. Such failings did little to erode his influence, however, and Aristotle remained the authority on animal structure, function, and natural history for nearly two thousand years.

Fascination with the unusual characterized much of the zoological literature produced during those two millennia. From Pliny the Elder's first-century description of lion/hyena hybrids, to Conrat von Megenberg's fourteenth-century mixture of dragon biology with fairly accurate observations of bees and eels, these writings sometimes mingle myths and facts. Then, between 1551 and 1555, the Swiss naturalist

Konrad von Gesner produced his own version of *Historia animalium,* which dealt primarily with European fauna and finally ended Aristotle's intellectual reign. But even von Gesner listed "species" that cannot be linked to known animals today, including, of course, the unicorn, which tradition demanded be discussed in any catalog of animals.

In the middle 1700s another Swiss, Carl von Linné (Linnaeus), whose grandfather had chosen a tree as the family name (Linné means "linden"), set about formally describing God's Kingdom. Although he didn't finish the task, he did devise a system for naming organisms. Implicit in Linnaeus's work is the idea that species are fixed entities, with features that define and distinguish them from all others. We know today that species are not fixed, that over time they evolve structural characters distinct from those of their ancestors. But what Linnaeus brought to science was a modern approach to anatomical research, along with a formal, and quite objective, method of organizing the observations.

Since Linnaeus's time, scientists have discovered and described thousands of new species. However, they have done this without being able to always agree on what a "species" actually is. "What is a species?" may be the most enduring question in biology. Sitting on the VSFS patio, thinking about the history of zoology and the Linnaean method, watching a single pelican soar for a while, join a couple of others in a flight around the bay, imitate the wing movements of one in front of it in formation, and finally settle on a beached panga, I translate this timeless biological question into a specific one: What is a brown pelican? And I know that in order to answer this question for myself, I must get my hands on a bird.

Theoretically, "more information" should help us answer both timeless and personal questions about the differences between types. However, additional knowledge sometimes makes distinctions disappear. If I knew the full history of pelicanlike birds, neither my single individual pelican nor its kind would seem particularly unique. In fact, the living animals would appear to be representative of a long progression of similar types. If we had thirty thousand pelican specimens in a museum, one for every century of the three million years pelicans have been on earth, and decided to count the number of species represented, the arbitrariness of our taxonomic decisions would be obvious even to any nonscientist. A child would look at the specimens laid out in rows and ask, with the same honesty as a fellow biologist: How did you decide where to draw the line between kinds?

Nor would the question — what is a brown pelican? — be completely resolved by taking the birds into the lab, where chemists could examine their molecules, even the DNA that in essence "spells" *Pelicanus occidentalis.* As part of the study a pelican gene could be put into a bacterium, that is, cloned, then analyzed in terms of its chemical detail, or "sequenced." The scientist could show you a protein made by bacteria using a brown pelican gene and say, "There, that is not the same kind as you'd expect to find in a white pelican." Or she could show you the results of the sequencing — long lists of letters made up of combinations of C, A, T, and G, abbreviations of the molecules in genes — and show you the places where the white pelican's list was different from that of the brown.

But where in those columns of letters are the migratory patterns of the two animals, behaviors that send the white into the interior of North America, while generally restricting the brown to the coasts? Only real pelicans, not lists of letters or pelican/bacteria proteins, glide low, wingtips barely missing the water, toward fishing boats fighting Baja's offshore winds. And where in that magnificent collection of thirty thousand specimens — one per century for the history of pelicans — or in that published table of triplets made from C, A, T, and G, can I find the individual variations so obvious among the birds now landing and carefully folding up their wings a few yards from where I sit on the field station patio?

In the twenty-three hundred years between Aristotle's time and today, the world's animals have not evolved nearly as much as our ideas about them. Most of the change in our point of view has come from the use of new techniques and equipment: spectrophotometers, gas chromatographs, electron microscopes, methods of chemical analysis, statistics — all little more than novel means of making observations. Technological powers have multiplied to such an extent that their application demands a philosophical analysis, a backing away from the practice of science, for a look at what science is doing to the manner in which we perceive the world. Slowly and surely our thinking is being directed toward the most fundamental level of life: DNA. Elected officials rarely understand technical jargon, so scientists have learned to speak politicese, expressing environmental concerns in terms of national security and economics. Thus the species being destroyed faster than we can discover them in the tropics are described in terms of their DNA, which might be useful in fighting human diseases or solving agricultural problems, rather than as raucous bright birds and fruity plants with rich smells and odd, almost embarrassingly Latin, names.

What has been gained in this evolution of viewpoint is mainly the politician's ear. What has been lost, on the other hand, is the mysticism, the wonder, of unanswerable questions about animals, for example: Why do brown pelicans glide so close to the water? Maybe the exotic mysteries have not died out but have been relegated to refugia, living, like tuataras on the islands of New Zealand's Cook Strait, in the minds of old zoologists. Maybe the questions thrive, or at least come out of hiding, when anachronisms walk down a beach two hundred miles from the nearest telephone and pick up shells, or gather in a cantina and talk about shark guts and tapeworms and the most difficult books anyone has ever read or written, or sit for hours on a stone wall and watch pelicans pick around in their feathers, or ask one another why, of all the birds out on the rocks, the brown pelican seems to be the most awkward yet at the same time the most graceful.

What has also been "gained" as a result of our scientific sophistication is a preoccupation with proximal questions, those beginning with the word "how," as opposed to ultimate questions, which are typically introduced by "why." Proximal problems deal with function, while ultimate ones address origins. The solutions to proximal problems provide us with power; if we know how something works, we can usually manipulate its operation, stopping it or making it work faster. The "best" politicians, as well as businessmen, coaches, and military leaders, extend this principle to human resources; engineers use it on machines.

Instead of power, the answers to ultimate questions give us understanding. The thirty thousand specimens in our imaginary museum would tell us many things about pelicans, including parts of their history we might never have inferred from studying extant birds. But this additional knowledge gives us no power. We can't make a brown pelican catch more fish, fly faster, glide closer to the water, spend less time dozing or preening, defecate more guano, or bend to our will in other ways, just by knowing what its ancestors looked like. What we can do with this information, instead, is make an educated guess about the way environmental factors force permanent changes on organisms. That guess would in turn lead to predictions about the fate of species in certain habitats. But maybe I've been too harsh in my assessment of the utility of research on ultimate questions. An elected leader who decided, after reading biologists' predictions, to save a species would need to draw heavily on the powers of insight and understanding to accomplish his or her goal.

But most of all, the historical knowledge might help us explain where, in the evolutionary sense, these seemingly bizarre and ungainly animals came from. The world is filled with highly successful but ugly "organisms." Some are bureaucracies; others are totalitarian states; a few are parasitic machines; a large, sad number are built of interpersonal relationships. Government agencies, computers, and love affairs are not literally, of course, organisms. But they do seem to garner energy, interact with their environments, and proliferate in a manner analogous, if not homologous, to pelicans. They evolve. Their ancestors and intermediate forms become extinct. Now we look around at the world we have built and see only the end products of this evolution.

Some scientists feel that the present array of life is largely a product of chance (see Stephen Jay Gould's *Wonderful Life*). According to this line of thought, had some now-extinct basic body plans survived, earth would be inhabited by a fauna so foreign to our present-day eyes that the animals would seem to have been imported from another planet. And indeed they would be from "another planet," one whose occupants might not include human beings. Many biologists claim that vicariance, that is, the splitting of populations due to continental drift or other geological events, has had more of an effect on large-scale evolutionary events than has natural selection. But we all agree that individual species occur only once. Destroy all brown pelicans and they are gone forever. Erase Baja California and it will never appear again. Millions of years hence earth may again have a bird or a mammal or a ??? that fills the pelican's niche, and may again have a desert land by the sea for that creature to live in, but those future animals and places will also be singularities. They will not be brown pelicans, and they will not be in the frontier state of Mexico.

In recent years scientists have started to develop ways of distinguishing features "of historical origin" from those considered "derived," the former being characteristic of ancestors, the latter acquired when species diverge from one another. Thus brown pelicans have a throat pouch because the group of birds to which pelicans belong has throat pouches. A legitimate scientific case could probably be made for the assertion that a pelican's pouch is large because its bill is long. But not all long-billed species have pouches; therefore the pelican's might have resulted from a peculiar development of the ventral notch of the lower mandible. So the intellectual problem becomes one of explaining the origin of bill structure instead of explaining the most distinctive feature, the pouch.

Thus my pelican sleeping on the blackened boulder near the low-tide line becomes a symbol of misdirected vision, of the easy ways we're fooled by looking only at what strikes us as unusual — distinctive instead of basic. Shifting my attention from a single individual to all the others up and down the shore, I think: My knowledge of this species is definitely incomplete, and although it ranges from Dixon Merritt's 1910 limerick ("A wonderful bird is the pelican") to memories of a Walt Disney film *(Water Birds),* in fact it is a mixture of truth and romance. What a privilege it would be to actually catch one of these birds, to experience in an afternoon the entire history of classical zoology — observation to mystic fascination to dissection and description — on a personal scale. Within hours, I get my wish.

Out on the bay, exploring the islands, Rafe spots something floating a quarter of a mile away. Biologists are intensely interested in animal debris; they study road kills at sixty-five miles an hour, assessing which ones are worth disrupting highway traffic for. So almost instinctively Rafe turns toward the brown blob. A few moments later he cuts the engine. I lean over the side and slip my hand under the wing. With the pelican on my lap, I work the neck and legs: no rigor mortis, the eye is fairly clear. This animal has died within the hour. And as taught once by a deeply respected professor, I study individual feathers, trying to imagine the colors I would use to paint them, noting their texture. My fingers explore the almost furry neck; it feels more like a winter coat than a pelican. The pouch is soft, almost delicate. I imagine the interaction between this frail skin and a twisting fish.

On shore I do what any zoologist, especially a parasitologist, would do with a dead pelican: dissect it, study its internal anatomy, go through its feathers for lice and mites, look in its gut for tapeworms. Beneath the breast skin is a layer of connective tissue filled with air pockets that cushion the bird against the force of its dive. As my scissors slice through this layer, I'm reminded of the plastic bubble sheeting used to wrap electronic parts and small bottles of expensive chemicals. The brown pelican is extremely buoyant, riding very high on the water; the structural feature that helps it survive a feeding dive also makes it float.

But an adaptation that increases buoyancy also inhibits diving. It makes no difference whether these adaptations are structural or behavioral; they are still antagonistic. The pelican lives in a state of compromise. Rafe and I talk about the bird and speculate on the cause of death as it slowly comes apart, piece by piece, in my hands. I cannot find any large clots, hemorrhages, broken bones, or other obvious internal lesions. No fish spines or steel hooks penetrate its intestine. Its skull is not crushed.

"Maybe it just hit the water wrong," offers Rafe. "You see injured ones pretty often."

I'm a person who watches wildlife constantly. Most of the dead birds I see are on streets or highways, below nests, and at the bases of buildings with large glass windows. One fresh brown pelican floating on Bahía de los Ángeles seems an anomaly. But a year later, at almost the same place, I get my hands on another pelican, this one still alive.

"It didn't fly," says one of the students. "It just sat there." She points to the intertidal boulders where she had been studying something down between the rocks. "We shooed it up in the weeds."

I walk a hundred yards across the sand and stop in front of a brown pelican that stares up at me, its head pulled down between its wings. I grab the bill with my left hand, simultaneously slipping the fingers of my right around the front edges of its wings. The bird struggles slowly; it weighs next to nothing, but the flight muscles don't feel particularly shrunken. Pelicans are mostly feathers.

Back in the station building, I give the pelican to a student, then dig out my watercolors. Handling a live, relatively large, wild animal is always a rare privilege. I never come away from the contact unchanged. Painting the creature's picture, especially in front of an audience, multiplies the impact of the encounter many times over. And so I sit on the couch, paint pan and glass of water on a chair beside me, a dozen faces watching, and begin to record the colors and textures of a single *Pelicanus occidentalis* picked up off the beach and held in the lap of a young woman who, like myself, had never touched a wild living pelican before that morning.

The pencil sketch complete, I begin painting with the most difficult color, a small swash of red on the bill, which is finely textured and mottled, an extremely complex visual challenge. Bird reds are very deceptive; to render them in watercolor requires experience, an eye that sees through surface appearances, patience, and luck. Experience comes only from making mistakes over a period of years; I've done that, but with the living animal staring at me, I wonder whether I have done it enough. The required vision may have to be inherited. Patience is forced upon me because the paint must dry, even on a small area, before I can tell whether I have mixed the colors correctly. And luck? This last is really a question of whether I've brought the right pigments to Mexico.

Two hours later I hold the picture at arm's length. The student takes the pelican back to the beach. The next day it is gone. Over the next few days I study the picture, propped up against the wall in a back room of the VSFS building. The bird watches me, still communicating some stoic tolerance of a fate it had no option but to accept. But the pouch is not done well. The paint does not convey the texture of that fine skin. Color and texture are so inextricably linked in nature that if you let those two attributes drift apart from one another, you lose the sense of wildness. That is, you have to paint what a bird *feels* like as well as what it looks like.

As I study the painting, the problem of explaining the origin of *Pelicanus occidentalis* as a type seems to be one of discovering the environment that best combines the colors and textures of the bird. A trip to the islands of Bahía de los Ángeles provides the opportunity to do just that. When they leave the intertidal boulders, pelicans often fly far out over the water, disappearing into the horizon's jagged profile of reds and purples. We follow them to the places where they nest and roost in the off-season — twisted basalt piles and ledges covered with dried guano, below the scorched tops of isolated crags.

Rafe again cuts the engine and we drift past the scene. Never have I seen an animal's colors and patterns fit so completely into a physical space. The subtle yet highly variable colors of the furlike neck feathers are trails of dried pelican manure on volcanic rock. The bill line and shadow are a crevice. The feathers that cover the back of the wing lie like the seams where molten lava ran hot, then cooled and dried, and finally was pushed until it folded and cracked. Of all the places these birds have been in the past few hours, none so perfectly matches and complements their appearance as does this rocky island. Suddenly all of the brown pelican's features, even the enigmatic ones, the incongruities, make sense. This animal belongs on, and to, the islands. Visually it melts into the rocks.

At this point the pelican becomes a metaphor instead of a bird. As the boat sways, tossing with its own backwash and the waves pushed into the bay from the Gulf of California, the pelicans sit silent, motionless, watching us. The longer I look, the more pelicans appear. Adjusting my "search image" allows me to see the hidden components of a scene; actively deciding what to seek instead of accepting the picture as presented to me reveals elements that would otherwise be invisible. But here alongside the Islas de los Gemelos we can test our higher levels of vision by learning how to observe pelicans in order to discover the significance of their colors and patterns. It is this last discovery that is at the heart of all scientific endeavor: We come to the Vermilion Sea not to find brown pelicans but to learn how to look for their properties.

9

The Gastropod's Gestalt

What is it? is the first question asked by a child taken to a museum or zoo. Prior to the "what is it?" stage, we exhibit the point and babble intelligible only to a proud parent. Later, as adults, we usually control ourselves — "It's not polite to point!" — but we still sometimes feel a quick rush of amazement when we encounter an exotic creature. Scientists learn to point in a dignified way — the grand sweeping gesture over a habitat, the directed movement of a laser beam across a screen full of numbers, the probe needle held steadily against an organ uncovered by dissection. But nobody is really fooled much by the theatrics we acquire with age and training. A point is still a point; no matter how heavily disguised, our verbal pontifications are still an expression of raw wonder. "Look at that!" we are saying. Our explanations are then answers to the "what is it?" that finally, after all these years and all this work, have been revealed to us.

Modern biology struggles mightily with the three-word question, possibly because of the cultural evolution of an American science driven largely by military and political power and economics. Thus sometimes a student who is perfectly at ease with complex biochemical analyses, but does not know what a crayfish is, is assigned to teach a freshman biology lab. At the national level expertise in the identification of obscure animals dies off faster than it can be replaced from the supply of oddball intellects that seem to appear, predictably but rarely, among university student populations. Research collections, time, and literature — the museum resources needed to finish the catalog of earthly species — slide inexorably down the list of government budgetary priorities. Nobody gets a patent on a tropical beetle, no fat royalty checks get deposited in foundation accounts from the publication of faunal and floral lists, and a four-page description of a parasitic worm costs, rather than pays, the author. But against this social landscape a professional biologist, one who *teaches* invertebrate zoology, can still squat on his heels in the receding afternoon tide of Bahía Concepción, with the distant island profiles turning into watercolors, and be totally consumed by the striking patterns of minute snails.

I walk out of the water, up to the windrow of debris that marks the high-tide line. Scattered among the many treasures are tiny shells, each with brilliant wavy lines straight out of the latest rock video. I hold a dozen specimens, turning them over and over in my palm, smiling. A bronzed woman in a blue swimsuit approaches, looks at me, than saunters over to peer into my collection.

"Huh," she says, "nerites." She and her husband are Canadians who, since their retirement, have spent October through March camped on a Mexican beach. She doesn't know that the Berlin Wall has fallen or that a Rumanian dictator and his wife have been executed; news of the shattering political upheavals in Eastern Europe has not reached the shores of Bahía Concepción. But she knows her snails. By sight, that is; if I asked her what a nerite *really* is, I suspect she'd give me a blank stare. She cannot describe the excretory and reproductive systems; "radula" is not in her vocabulary; "proso-branch," "mantle cavity," and "ctenidium" leave her shaking her head. These words refer to soft parts, which are usually missing from washed-up shells, and you don't have to remember much internal anatomy to be a collector.

I don't explore her malacological expertise further; she is retired and relaxed on the fine gravel washed with crystal water and has no use for textbook knowledge. Instead she exhibits a rather common behavior, namely, a "search for the best." Because of the resources available locally, that search is directed toward shells. She launches into a recitation of her friend's collecting exploits, tallying the cowries, various kinds of murexes, olives, cones, stories falling by the way like chipped specimens held only until the better one is found, then cast back upon the sand. These animals live as their secretions. The calcium prisms laid down with such precision function rather like a book that assumes its author's identity or a building that is called by an architect's last name rather than by the corporation that occupies it.

"Wait here," she says, "I have something to show you." She walks down the beach to her trailer, then returns with a small lion's paw pecten. "Do you know how old this is?"

I handle the little scallop gently; its colors are still true; on the large ridges the fine sculpturing is still intact. By virtue of past association with museum curators, I've had the opportunity to touch many similar items.

"Forty million years," I guess.

She looks at me suspiciously, as if being one-upped by a stranger wasn't in her plan for the day.

"Close."

Species of the genus *Lyropecten* (the lion's paw) have lived in Baja California, or what was to become that part of Mexico, since the Miocene. Volcanism, fault-block tilting, and erosion have changed the face of the landscape more rapidly than the molluscs have altered their basic shapes. A shell is a three-dimensional object whose shape is determined by DNA molecules that have been replicated, more or less faithfully, for millions of years. We walk down the beach, pick up shells, and assign them names based on the words and pictures printed together in a book. Then we repeat our identifications to friends and strangers. So long as we go uncorrected, our association between the name and the image is strengthened by repetition. We become an "expert in the identification of molluscs." Our friends, and the strangers we encounter, admire our "knowledge." After a few years we may forget the criteria we originally used to establish the relationship between a pattern and a word. And if we never dig deeply into the literature or conduct a lifetime of anatomical research, we have no idea whether the characters we recognize so easily are true reflections of a common evolutionary history, and thus of a genetic relationship, or are features acquired independently by fundamentally disparate forms.

Beneath my feet lies an enormously diverse population of shells, some from truly intertidal molluscs, others evidently washed up from deeper water. They represent one of the world's most accessible natural lessons on the subject "variations on a theme." For example, snail shells have an aperture, the opening through which the head and foot protrude during life. If the aperture is the "theme," variations on it include greatly elongated, partially closed, shoved to one end, drawn out into a canal, and toothed on the inside margin. Virtually all the basic features of shells — surface sculpturing, height of spiral, extent to which one whorl overgrows another — display similar diversity.

Differences suggest process. I kneel down among the nerites, sort through the *Nassarius,* select a series of bubbles and whelks, then align them on the sand in a row of supposedly progressive change. This need to place shells in sequence must be a deep-seated one; I do it almost without thinking, then smile at the results, and at my knowledge of what colleagues would say were they here, who-knows-how-many miles from the nearest telephone, a thousand times that far from the closest scientific journal, and light years apart from an audience that cares about fundamental errors in evolutionary thought.

Safe from peer review, on the shores of Bahía Concepción, I place one shell beside another, then add a third, and a fourth, until my snail sentence on the sand reads: "This is the history through which body whorls came to dominate, to overgrow all that has gone before, to hide the mistakes of youth, and to present full-formed adult beauty to a world that looks for treasures in the detritus of a beach." At one end of my line is a rock with a worm shell stuck to it; at the other end is a cowrie. *Vermicularia* — loose and undisciplined — is on the left; *Cypraea* — tightly self-contained, shiny, and spotted — is on the right. But this series tells more about *my* species than about gastropods. Cowries have been used as decorations and as commercial trade items for a long time; I don't remember reading about such value being placed on worm shells. Of course my snail sentence is laid out from left to right.

In his book *Wonderful Life*, Stephen Jay Gould begins with a discourse on the iconography of progress. He includes an illustration of "human evolution," a series of pictures purporting to show gradual change from ape through primitive ape-man to Neanderthal, Cro-Magnon, and finally "modern man," upright, well groomed, naked. If you were assigned the task of dressing the figure on the far right, you'd probably choose a dark business suit and a briefcase. Something in his posture suggests an appropriate wardrobe and accessories. The Neanderthal behind Cro-Magnon holds his weapon at his side, parallel to the ground, arm slightly curled. Would a gorilla hold a branch the same way? Probably. But Cro-Magnon has obviously progressed beyond the brute stage; he carries the spear jauntily, almost like a tennis racket slung casually over his shoulder, suggesting he's ready to talk first, maybe jaw a little bit about who paints the best bison on the cold stone walls of Altamira, then fight over an idea, or at least something more important than a dried mammoth haunch.

Such pictures are used in a multitude of ways. Harmlessly, a political cartoonist removes one of the "lesser" forms and inserts in its place a football player in the opposing team's uniform. Not so harmlessly, a best-selling introductory biology text, used in colleges and universities around the country, uses this same iconography, but in a much more subtle way. In the chapter on human evolution, we find a figure with three skeletons posed in a sylvan setting — a monkey on a branch at the far left, a gorilla slouched, left hand hooked around an overhanging limb, right knuckles dragging the ground, in the middle, and a human on the right. Even though the human is a skeleton, its arrangement is reminiscent of that seen in Andreas Vesalius's sixteenth-century medical engravings, that is, the posture says "elegant and civilized." Reading left to right, we interpret "progress" to be (1) abandonment of the trees, (2) assumption of erect posture, and (3) attainment of grace, accentuated by the contrast with the gorilla's hunched posture.

The major problem with this monkey–gorilla–person picture is that all the skeletons, like my shells on the beach, are *contemporaries.* In this same textbook, a second illustration shows full frontal nudes reconstructed from fossil skeletons or in some cases partial skeletons. At the left, three and a half feet tall, is "Lucy," the famous *Australopithecus afarensis* of Donald Johanson, and to the right of her are three rather obvious males of increasing height and good looks. Reading left to right, in the same sequence we follow as we progress through a sentence until we get its complete message, "advancement" seems to be associated with maleness in addition to increasing size.

In the same chapter a third illustration shows skulls, including several that were evidently contemporary one and a half to three million years ago, arranged in a sequence with Lucy on the left and *Homo sapiens sapiens* on the right. "Progress" is defined here as change from large face and small brain to small face and large brain, culminating with "wise wise man" (the literal translation of *H. sapiens sapiens*). If the freshman textbook I hold in my hand is correct, the modern hominoid that brought you the population explosion, clearing of tropical forests at a hundred acres a minute, and nuclear weapons is the wisest of the wise. On the beach at Bahía Concepción, amid the incredible variety of snail shells, I find myself wondering what kinds of stories can be told by selecting items and placing them in a sequence. For example, if progress is to be represented by a change toward delicacy, a tendency to become easily broken, smooth, difficult to transport far away to strange places in crude containers, my sequence is: *Cypraea annettae, Polinices bifasciatus, Oliva incrassata, Bulla gouldiana.* But if progress means becoming miniaturized, perhaps to hide away, to be discovered only by an observant and sensitive eye, or even to fit into a spacecraft, then I start with *Hexaplex erythrostomus,* follow with *Pteropurpura erinaceoides,* and end with *Nassarius tiarula.* If progress means a job, a good, solid, blue-collar job and a ticket to the ball game, calluses and swollen knuckles, and a toughness that defies even the tides, I can make any series, so long as it ends with *Cerithium;* their shells look rugged enough to withstand all sorts of physical abuse. If progress is manifested in diversity — once everyone wore animal skins, now the cable news flashes a kaleidoscope of color and style — then my row of shells leads to *Theodoxus luteofasciatus;* no two of their boldly striped patterns are the same. Thus I read the stories told by snails laid purposefully on the beach.

But in nature shells are not laid purposefully in a line. Instead they are washed up seemingly at random. However, each resting place is the temporary end point of a unique history. The *Theodoxus* in my hand is no less a singularity than a rock formation beneath my feet. Each had its beginning in an identifiable set of earthly events, repeated innumerable times but never in exactly the same way, never with exactly the same results. Orogeny — the building of mountains from volcanic explosions and the faulting and folding of the rock layers — is no less wondrous than ontogeny — the construction of an organism from a single cell. The bursts of DNA and protein synthesis are as dramatic as earthquakes or the eruptions of magma, and the involution of tissues is a morphogenetic process as inexorable as the recrystallization of sediments. Yet through it all a certain character persists — "nerite," "mountain" — the accepted names proof of the hidden power of pattern.

With single shells we are faced with exactly the same situation we found studying cacti on the desert, namely the problem of deciding which variations are of kinds as opposed to those of individual specimens. Confronted with the small sample of *Theodoxus luteofasciatus,* my lady friend on the beach didn't hesitate an instant before proclaiming "nerite." She recognized a pattern, properly included it within a class of patterns stored in her memory, then called up the right word not only for the group of related items but also for the occasion — chatting with a stranger on the beach about a handful of snail shells.

I wonder if she went through the same, almost unconscious, process with me, adjusting her perception to fit my appearance, demeanor, and collecting habits, then drawing upon her knowledge of the intertidal fauna to provide the context within which she chose her words. I was dressed conservatively for the beach — jeans and T-shirt — a fiftyish man with no earring, medium-length hair, not obviously into body building or surfing, with old-fashioned sunglasses and a fairly carefully selected set of shells in my left hand. I must have reeked of college professor. Therefore I received a "nerite" instead of a casual glance. She recognized my interest in invertebrates but couldn't accurately assess my level of knowledge from these visual clues. After all, I might have been a history professor. She knew I was not a skilled and serious shell collector simply because such a person would already have a whole series of nerites. But she suspected that I knew more about snails than the average person. And she was confident enough in her classification of me that she brought out her precious fossil.

It is precisely this highly flexible use of knowledge and experiences — information — that draws the line between artificial and true intelligence, between the most massive computers we can build and the woman on the beach who doesn't know the Berlin Wall has fallen but knows her snails, suspects that a stranger reads books, sometimes even non-fiction, and fashions these perceptions into an appropriately open-ended communication. And she does it faster than a supercomputer.

While *T. luteofasciatus* may be easily identifiable, it is also extraordinarily variable in color. Thus the formal scientific literature contains the words "with very variable, oblique stripes of gray, black, yellow, and white," and the common name — painted nerite — reflects this trait. In this case, shell structural features override particular colors as identifying marks. But extreme variability is a trait of some nerites and not others, so it can be thought of as a "metacharacter," that is, we use the range of colors in the same way we would use a single color if it were stable.

Identification criteria must also be applied within a broader context; for example, it is often important to know where a specimen was collected. The specific colors and patterns of another nerite, *Neritina virginea,* from the West Indies, are as variable as those of *T. luteofasciatus.* The sizes, shapes, and textures of the shells are also similar, but the two species live in different oceans. However, the context can also be an intellectual environment, a supply of ideas, knowledge, and experience that helps us subconsciously sort through characters, keeping some, discarding others. I could tell a museum malacologist the other kinds of shells that were part of a collection, and he or she could immediately eliminate large numbers of related forms from a list of species to which the unknown snail might belong.

All organisms have such suites of characteristics that tend to occur together, for example, habitat, associated species, physiological adaptations, behavioral traits, body proportions. In an instant, the trained eye "sees" in animals not only these properties, but also a scientific name, a nested hierarchy of increasingly inclusive categories — families, orders, classes — to which the specimen belongs, the nature of variation typical of a genus, the evolutionary history of the family, the geographical distribution of the order, literature telling who described this species, when, and in what publication, and any subsequent research that has been done on the group.

The journal articles are particularly revealing. Formal biological studies fall into four general categories: catalog/descriptive, proximal, ultimate, and exemplary. The vast majority of animals are represented in the scientific and technical literature only by descriptions or notes of occurrence, as on faunal and floral lists or in natural histories of an area. Elaborate and extensive, this body of writing, drawing, measurement, and comparison is directed toward our original question: What is it? Several hundred new species descriptions are published every year, evidence that scientists are still a long way from discovering what plants and animals share earth with us. Most politicians, businessmen, and other "leaders" do not know such activity exists; typically they are completely unaware of the monumental ignorance that characterizes our intellectual relationship with the planet upon which our children live.

The scientific literature is also filled with research papers on both function and origin, addressing proximal and ultimate questions, respectively, but the list of species so studied is relatively short. Only when we begin to ask parallel questions about the questions themselves do we understand the vital link between these two types of inquiry. Thus we have not only a snail in the hand but also a testable hypothesis, in our head, about regulation of body fluid chemical makeup in intertidal gastropods, as well as a preliminary explanation for the evolutionary diversification of littoral molluscs in general. The ideas in this case are as real as the animal. Now let us ask the proximal and ultimate questions not about the nerite but about the *hypotheses:* How do they work? and, where do they come from?

The relative values of questions about function vs. those concerning origin are reversed when we step up a level from biology to metabiology — the study of biology as a discipline. Testable hypotheses are tools used in formal research; they also serve as criteria by which we distinguish scientific from nonscientific explanations for natural phenomena. But when we ask the ultimate question — where do hypotheses come from? — suddenly we see how important it is not to solve problems but to find problems, not to falsify assertions but to make them, for to a scientist, a world without questions is like a beach without shells.

The final class of formal studies — the exemplary ones — is the rarest. Here we find the intellectual equivalents of *Murex elenensis* or a perfect four- to five-inch *Turritella*. In a library, among the metaphorical worn sand grains, the battered foraminiferan tests, chips of urchin spine, flakes of oyster shell, there appears, to the sharpest collector's eye, the "classic piece," a combination of discovered problem and designed solution that illustrates the upper limit of elegance in science. Our researcher has walked for miles, and years, spoken to campers on the beach, picked over shells in curio shops, kept some specimens, thrown most away, always asking "What is it?" He or she is looking for some truly unusual combination of insight and experience applied to a puzzle whose solution shows us the ideal approach. These are the investigations that will be collected by teachers and deposited in the museum of introductory textbooks to show the general public what is meant by the word "biology."

On the beach at Bahía Concepción, I pocket a few *Theodoxus luteofasciatus;* everyone should have some. But I keep on walking, looking for that perfect example of how snail shells are made, a quest that leads naturally to a wondering about all the possible ways shells could be made. And back in the winter classroom a month later, a universe away from the Sea of Cortés, having seen what a mindless gastropod has built from calcium salts, I look at my audience and can't help but apply the symbolism of snail shells to the business at hand. I ask: How *should* the next few weeks of our interaction be designed? How can I shape the raw materials of my profession into the perfect specimen lecture that each of my students will take home and, like the lady in the blue swimsuit, present to a stranger who seems to be looking for something?

10

El Coyote

———————

In the darkness, upon a beach called El Coyote, a ring of people huddle close to fire. They have gathered wood with great effort, for the creeping tide laps against a desert land in which there are few trees. A day earlier, miles to the north, they collected some dead *datilillos,* tree yuccas, but scorpions sulked in the foamy dried cores, and these "logs" burned so quickly that the chill soon returned, and the people wished for a stack of familiar oak or hickory. But on this night, those staring into the flames enjoy the results of their afternoon's labor: They've found some mesquite and an ironwood tree that has already been burned once; a trash fire stripped off its leaves and twigs, and the people hacked for a long time to cut the remaining branches and drag them into camp. In the flickering yellow light they joke, sip chocolate, and sing.

Then out of the night a stranger walks into the circle of light and stands in their midst. He grins up at the faces, showing his wrinkles, and gaps where teeth used to be. He has no coat, only a heavy shirt, brown pants and canvas shoes with no socks. His forehead and his lips are seared by the sun. When he speaks, his voice is rough, slurred, throaty, hoarse with a nasal twang. The people around the fire suspect he has been drinking.

"*¿Cerveza?*"

We shake our heads; we have no *cerveza*.

"No *cerveza*."

"*¿Cerveza?*"

"No *cerveza*."

He looks around, squinting into the fire.

"*¿No cerveza?*" he asks again, more in disbelief than in affront. He shuffles over to the kitchen boxes and pokes through them to confirm our claim, then returns to the fire, sits down on the sand, and puts his hands to the heat. He inches his way in as close as he can to the flames without setting himself on fire.

"*¡Caliente!*" He grins and coughs.

"*Mucho caliente,*" we agree. Then someone plays the guitar, and the stranger smiles his gap-toothed smile and nods in time to the music. He stares at us, one by one, and gestures at the black dog that a few hours earlier simply walked in, as he himself did. We can tell from the look on the stranger's face that he knows — better than we, and we know well from just a few days' experience — that the hours ahead will be very cold. The dry wind will come out of the rocky, crumbling mountains behind us, a chilling, cutting wind that pounds on the tents. Then another wind will come, this one from out over the bay, and it too will be cold, but wet and salty. The ironwood fire will be dead, and those awakened by the cold will lie staring into the darkness. They will remember that the stranger had no coat or blanket, for he has rowed from an island, and all he has brought are the clothes he wears, his boat, and his fishing line.

Down the beach to the south lies a jagged, dark, rocky point. Below the high-tide line the boulders are covered with oysters, their razor-edged, serrated shells making it imperative not to stumble while searching through the shallows for periwinkles and tiny crabs. I also stare into the fire, like the stranger, and wonder how old he was when he first learned that oysters are sharp and can slice a hand that pokes too carelessly among them. His practical knowledge of bivalves must be deeply rooted in early childhood; all along the gulf coast, Mexican children dig clams beside their parents. A laboratory exercise in malacology lies scattered along the beach. Among the shells is a philosophical discourse on what it means to be a member of a highly variable species, or to be washed up before reaching your full potential, or to be drilled by a predator snail.

Beneath the obvious remnants of this great and thriving molluscan community are the microscopic pieces of another, hardly visible one, for the "sand" upon which we sit consists of tiny shell parts, pieces of urchin spines, and the like. The wave action ground these chips together, wearing them smooth and often unrecognizable, the physical forces of nature thus turning them into puzzles that grow more and more difficult to solve with each cycle of the moon. I wonder if the stranger knows, or even senses, the microscopic world beneath him, or ever thinks about how mountains turn to sand and how the urchins get ground up by the waves, also into what we call sand. Is his understanding of the natural world limited to what he needs to get a meal? Or could he tell us much about oysters, if we could understand him?

Around the campfire we try the native tongue, but we don't have enough words, and our conversation begins and ends with *cerveza*, a sorry commentary indeed upon American middle-class education, made sorrier by the fact that some of us have "taken Spanish" and others have brought their books. But somehow the formal schooling and the books fail when tested against the real thing: a live Mexican from out on the Sea of Cortés. Finally I venture a word that has stuck in my mind from previous encounters with people who chase fishes. "*¿Pescadero?*" I say, meaning "*pescador*" but not knowing that's what I mean. The mistake makes no difference.

His head snaps up; he nods, then gazes suspiciously — an old dog with cataracts, sore in the joints, whose sense of smell was still sharp. *Pescadero* has obviously struck deeply.

"*¿Tiburones?*"

He laughs.

"Sharks!" His one English word — "Sharks!" He laughs again, rocks back and forth at the fire, rubbing his hands. "Sharks!" he says to the sand, then "Sharks!" to the fire.

"*Tiburones.*" We pass the word around. The gulf is full of *tiburones* and, I know, the *tiburones* are full of worms, tiny and delicate worms with elaborate "heads," which live nestled in the elaborately folded lining of a shark's intestine.

I know these worm facts because a friend has told them to me. She came to the gulf a few years earlier on vacation, and brought a companion, a man who was very observant and didn't know what he wanted to be when he grew up. The vacation was ended by sharks. They strolled the beach at Puertecitos, where the *pescadors* were bringing in a variety of chondrichthians, including skates and rays. My friend asked for some intestines. People in her profession make such requests routinely, knowing that to be thought an idiot by Mexican fishermen is a small price to pay for exotic tapeworms. Her companion chuckled, shook his head, and went down the street looking for Tecate. Free shark guts, he knew, spelled the end of whatever "vacation" they had at first envisioned.

She spent the rest of the trip cutting up sharks, skates, rays, and guitars. He looked at the scenery and talked, as best he could, with local people. He wondered what he could do with his "vacation" while she collected worms, and he decided to collect impressions and ideas. Then he could write a book.

Or maybe several books. I met my friend and her companion years later, almost by chance, in Bahía de los Ángeles. She was fishing for sharks and having very little luck. He was fishing for material and having a great deal of luck. He complained, however, that his material wasn't selling. People think it's fiction, he said, frustrated. If they think it's fiction, I offered, then write it as fiction. Then he said he was having a great vacation because they weren't able to catch any sharks. So we all went down to Guillermo's and had some Tecate and some margueritas and some Santo Tomas wine and talked about shark tapeworms and about writing books that turned out to be something other than what we had intended them to be.

Small twigs with thorns still clutter the sand around the fire. Periodically someone picks up a sticker and throws it into the flames — a cleansing, almost vengeful, act against the potential a dead mesquite branch has for piercing a sneaker and the foot inside. The black dog doesn't notice the spines; he has evidently put his rear end down into so many over the years that he has become immune. The handsome mongrel pushes his way into the circle of warmth, his eyes bright and satisfied at the hands rubbing on his neck.

Nobody rubs the fisherman's neck. Instead we listen to him talk, understanding little, but trying to sense what he is trying to tell us. His tone is borderline emotional, not quite excited, but insistent. He gestures emphatically, coughing, his hoarse narrative obviously a personal, maybe even a professional, story. We smile, nod, laugh when he laughs. Finally, maybe in frustration, he picks up a stick and draws a picture in the sand: a straight line crossed, at regular intervals, by short curved ones. Suddenly the conversation makes sense. He has been talking about his boat; the picture is his "trot line." He fishes with hooks strung out on a long line. *"Pesca-*

dero" was indeed the key to an easily unlocked door. "Fish-monger" is evidently close enough to "fisherman," and it is not only what he does but what he is.

Then, as I have seen happen before when people assume that others can't understand what is being said, we talk about the fisherman in front of his face, as he is telling his tale. How powerful a tool is language, I think not only for freeing, but also for isolating and imprisoning us: Some male scientists go out with their wives but talk about experiments, and the wives talk about children, and suddenly the men feel they have missed something important that happened while they were at work. Even the simplest jargon contains implications only the in-group appreciates; for this reason, seemingly casual talk can serve to dehumanize the uninitiated. Argot defines self and nonself in terms of who understands and who does not.

I study the *pescador* through the flames, frustrated by my inability to communicate much with him, and I think about my own children, about how their fates may be dictated by the ignorance of my generation. A politician goes to Latin America and talks about "democracy! democracy! democracy!" when, in fact, if Baja California is any indication of the world beyond our borders, he should be talking about "old cars! old cars! old cars!" Will there be time for people who can sit around a fire and discuss boats with a Mexican fisherman to come into positions of great political power? Will there be time for a young man or woman who is willing to sit and watch a man draw a picture of his fishing line in the sand at midnight to grow up to be president? Such are the thoughts that come into a parent's mind, looking into a fire and seeing only lost time, lost opportunities, regardless of what else has been won.

"In the morning," says Rafe, "we should all go down and see his boat." Rafe describes the battered wooden boat pulled up on the rocks half a mile to the north as the fisherman continues talking about his lines. "And when we get back to Bahía de los Ángeles, we should all sit down together and read *The Pearl*. It only takes an hour to read."

I grow tired of the fireside conversations that never seem to reach a conclusion I can understand. In my sleeping bag, adjusting bone and flesh once more to the Mexican ground, I listen to the stranger talk well into the night. His voice becomes happier but more insistent. I decide that he thinks he is making progress, but that progress is measured as very simple realizations following many minutes of exchange. Then, periodically, I hear familiar words, touched, nevertheless, with a little wonder, the spice of discovery: forty years, *cuarenta años,* he has lived on the beach. Forty years! But lying on the sand, listening, watching the fire cast yellow light on the tent, I am suspicious of what we have discovered through talking in two different languages. Has he really lived on the beach for forty years? Or on the island? Or has he been rowing over here to ask *gringos* for *cerveza* every night for the last forty years? Or is he forty years old? I smile and go to sleep listening to this discussion held around a fire I know will soon die out.

Suddenly I am awake. The wind has stopped. The chill has made rivulets of condensation on the cloth a few inches above my face, and out over the water gulls call, their voices bouncing off the rocks. They know, simply because they were hatched knowing, that dawn is not long away. Then I hear a cough, and the oars — wood against wood making a sound not unlike the gulls' calls. Far out in the bay, the stranger rows and coughs, rows and coughs. I listen for what seems to be an hour, as the various sounds of Bahía Concepción paint a picture in my mind: postcard blue against a white/tawny beach curving gently to the basalt rocks and the crumbling ocher hills behind. On the tallest cardon a vulture spreads its wings to warm and dry the frosty dew. No blowing plastic bags litter this image, no stripped and rusted Fords, only the gentle wake of a wooden boat and the swirls made by long oars. In the predawn orange a line of porpoises heads north. I unzip the tent flap, watch their distant, silent, arching dark-finned backs, and think only of the eons it must have taken for such a wondrous body to evolve. The second time, that is. A hundred million years ago I could have stood upon a similar beach somewhere, seen an almost identical sight, and thought the same thoughts, but called the animals ichthyosaurs instead of porpoises.

The camp stirs; sounds of a Coleman stove being fired and a charred blue metal coffee pot being filled mix with the squabbling of gulls. The black dog bounds down the beach, followed at a distance by a man. I forget what name we have given this dog — is this one Lobo, or was Lobo what we called that dingolike beast that plopped his generic canine frame down on a tent flap and went to sleep at San Ignacio? The black one wasn't Handlicker or Mutt; those, I remember distinctly, were the dogs we tossed pancakes to at Bahía de los Ángeles. Somehow the irresistible — instinctive? — urge of young people to name dogs makes more of an impression on me than the names themselves. Do dogs name people, or simply distinguish between those who toss scraps and those who don't? The man walking up the beach is Mario, the proprietor of the El Coyote campsite. He must be the one who supplied the two boards laid over the sunken barrel inside the duck blind called an outhouse. Unlike the fisherman, Mario speaks English, laced liberally with California slang.

"You doin' okay?" asks Mario. We talk about the morning, the beauty of the sunrise, and about the stranger from the night before. "Hope you didn't give him any beer," laughs Mario. "Give 'im beer and you'll never get rid of 'im!"

"He said he fished for sharks."

"Oh!" Mario laughs again, shakes his head. "He usually brings in a coupla three fish." He gestures up and down the beach. "Tries to sell 'em. Sometimes he rows up to Mulegé."

"His name, Mario, we never asked him his name." Twenty Americans had spent four hours learning that the man was a fisherman, but hadn't asked him his name. Nor had we given him a name, the way we did the dogs.

"Kino," says Mario. "That's old Kino. Hope you didn't give him any beer."

At Bahía de los Ángeles, the Vermilion Sea Field Station library contains the complete works of John Steinbeck as well as other treasures, such as the transcript of a TV documentary about a Bob Dylan tour of England. The Steinbeck books are mostly paperbacks, present in multiple copies, all well thumbed. I choose the most intact edition of *The Pearl*. I remember the story well: A Mexican baby is bitten by a scorpion, and the child's incredibly poor parents have no money to pay the arrogant and wealthy physician. The young father, an oyster fisherman, works frantically to find a pearl worth the price of the doctor's help. But the gigantic pearl, when he finally collects it, brings nothing but sorrow and violence to the young family. In the end, the man throws the pearl back into the Sea of Cortés.

What I had not remembered about Steinbeck's story was that the young father's name was Kino.

In some ways the boundary separating Kino's life from ours is as sharp and nonnegotiable as that between the intertidal rocks and the barren red hills behind Bahía Concepción. And the inhabitants of those respective environments reflect the physical differences of the landscapes: the loose red dirt, weathered dry rocks, and scattered cacti above, the shell gravel, oyster-encrusted boulders, masses of snails, and brittle stars beneath weathered stones below. Yet a scientist can walk from knee deep in the cold waves, through the mangroves, and up into the rock crevices decorated with petroglyphs in only a few minutes, calling upon knowledge and experience to give his mind access to these different communities along the way.

It is not so easy with the *pescador*; the evolutionary histories that separate cardon from the intertidal polychaetes are as divergent and irreversible in the biological sense as those separating us from Kino are in the cultural sense. Although the time over which life gave rise to both worms and cacti is vastly longer than that required to produce both fishermen and college students, the results are equivalent. As much as we appreciate his company, and interact with him as best we can, none of us can ever *become* such a man. While we may learn his colloquial Spanish, catch as many fish as he, and spend as many nights asking tourists for beer, we can never live his childhood or grow up in his parents' home. But understanding of, and respect for, that which we know we do not know stimulates our curiosity about biotic communities. This interest in turn drags our attention along, demanding that curiosity be satisfied. And, I suspect, this same respect will tell us to ask a stranger his name next time, just as we so often ask our teacher, What is this species?

11

To Build a Museum

We spent several days on the beach at El Coyote. I came to see clearly how a total preoccupation with intertidal life, in a setting of such incomparable beauty, could distance a person from nearly all worldly concerns. Sometime in the days following our visit to Bahía Concepción, Rafe, Glen, and I talked about the intrigue of pure exploration. I told of my visits to paleontological digs, where all who entered the marked-off, trenched areas suddenly focused their full attention on the next fossil, and where helpers spent hours completely absorbed in the washing of clay and the collection of microscopic teeth. Then we bemoaned the difficulty of providing opportunities for students simply to go study natural history in rich and exciting places. Travel is expensive and time-consuming, political instability denies us access to many areas of the world, and most of all, the expertise needed to provide guidance is often in short supply. Yet I knew from experience that there were ways to make nature available to almost anyone "off the street." What I didn't know was that in Bahía de los Ángeles, a town without a telephone, an effort was being made to do just that.

"Let's take a walk," says Rafe one morning, not long after our return from Bahía Concepción. "I want to show you the town."

We set out after breakfast, joined by the ever-present dogs. A week before, we had arrived at the Vermilion Sea Field Station in the moonless night, then left for points south early the next day. In the late evening the thick darkness hid everything except some rows of yellow windows through which I saw people sitting at tables. Then the walls of the van closed in; tamarisk branches blew, dancing like ghosts through the stabbing headlights; the hard jolt of large stones under the wheels and the barking of dogs were what I first felt and heard in this town that had come to mean so much to Raphael Payne.

Now, in the morning light, I shield my eyes against the glare from stucco and unpainted concrete blocks. The Ocañas' auto and truck repair business lies scattered almost to my feet; every rusted old Ford I have ever owned, asleep, in peace at last, sits tilted slightly on blocks or rims gouging into the sand. Piles of mussel shells — the remnants of somebody's dinners — lie along the wall separating small verandas from the narrow alley that serves as an entrance into the field station. The dogs that were so excited last night walk between and around us, almost nonchalantly, licking their lips and looking up at us.

"The station building itself was the headquarters for the mining company." Rafe points out the rusting abandoned equipment — beams and pulleys, another example of the massive machinery necessary for modern humans to move large amounts of rock, salt, water, other machines, or, for that matter, people.

Commercial and military installations — in San Diego, Ensenada, anywhere — bristle with cranes, A-frames, and overhead railings. The old salt pier at Guerrero Negro oxidizes away, covered with gull droppings and graffiti, watched over by a vacant lighthouse with crumbling rooms at its feet. And at Bahía de los Ángeles, evidence of the extinct mining operation lies scattered, sometimes subtly, sometimes not, among the houses and up into the mountains. Large gears and shafts rest, half buried in the sand; heavy metal panels — bin or hopper pieces? — lean against buildings; pieces of massive cable are seen here and there, like tired old snakes trying to hide under boxes or slip beneath a sheet of twisted corrugated roofing.

In my mind I try to reconstruct all this stuff, asking what the miners did with it and how they used it. But only the little engine, sitting on a pedestal in the town square, and the old ore cars, their patina not unlike that of desert stones, exhibit obvious functions. I stare at these artifacts with a certain amount of awe. They are not particularly fine machines. Technology may have made it possible to dig for gold in the hills above the Bay of Angels, but not even tracks and wheels could have made it easy.

"Papa Diaz died last year; he was the patriarch of one of the old Bahía families. The town lost one of its major historical figures. The older Ocaña, Arnulfo, also died." Up on a veranda in the Diaz compound, children laugh and bounce with excitement; a birthday-party bubbling of little voices washes down and through the otherwise silent town. The piñata takes its blows, dancing, recoiling, but not breaking. My first exposure to Hispanic culture was as a small child in Oklahoma City, visiting my grandfather. The family next door had no tree in their yard, so they used my grandfather's gnarled old pear tree to hang the piñata. I got my futile turn with the stick. The birthday boy broke it handily. His name was Johnny Diaz. Forty-five years later I am walking by a Diaz party. In all the hours I spent playing games with Johnny, I never asked him anything about Mexico. I probably didn't know there was a Mexico.

"Before Guillermo had a cantina, sometimes we'd stop in Casa Diaz or Las Hamacas for a beer." Rafe points out the field biologist's landmarks — watering holes where a day's wonders are cataloged and evaluated so they'll be remembered.

"This is a word-of-mouth society," Rafe says. "It doesn't take long for people to find out that a foreigner is a college professor."

When you study clams as well as eat them, drive the coastal desert roads looking for places to bring students, and ask sport fishermen if they have seen any whales, before long the questions start flowing toward you instead of away. I've had the same experience in small Nebraska towns, where strangers in a bar often are inspected, shaved of their anonymity, then grilled. I'm asked biological questions as often in establishments with names like "The Sip 'n' Sizzle" as I am in class; I feel it is as important to give an interesting answer in one place as in the other.

"Once in a while the bikers would come in from places like Bahía de las Animas," continues Rafe. The Bay of Spirits is down the coast along one of the trails bikers choose over highways. "They'd start telling how whales came right up close to the beach. Of course the fishermen weren't going to be outdone with tall tales, so they'd say, 'Yeah, and five thousand porpoises went by the boat.'" It takes very little of this kind of conversation, even in an American bar, before people begin looking to a biology teacher for answers. They want to know what it was they *really* saw, and after a couple of beers they will gladly use your authority to embellish their stories back home. "So the biologists got to thinking, maybe you could get a lot of information, you know, *useful* information, if you could find a way to take advantage of all these people out on the water. And we all wanted the tourists to appreciate the marine life they were seeing."

"Useful" information in biology consists of nonrandom, patterned observations, typically of some plant or animal species you're interested in. Such sightings either disrupt or complement your picture of the natural world; they are never neutral. Scientists spend spectacular amounts of time, money, and creativity in search of useful information. They design Orwellian contraptions, recruit enthusiastically gullible doctoral students, write novel-like grant proposals, and sell their souls to government and industry for financial support. Rafe and his colleagues figured you wouldn't have to do all that if you had fishermen and tourists at your disposal.

Mexico Highway 1 was blacktopped in the early 1970s. Pretty soon thousands of tourists were coming down; Baja California was literally opened up. Prior to the paving, most vacationers had neither the will nor the vehicles to negotiate hundreds of miles of boulder-strewn desert upon which black cattle stood at night. Bahía de los Ángeles had always been a popular place for sport fishermen, but along with the fresh asphalt came new fishermen — Americans mostly — some driving trucks with a deep freeze and a Honda generator in the back and pulling every conceivable kind of boat. They would go out into the bay and come back with a load of thirty-pound yellowtail, which they would clean and drop into the freezer. After a few days of fishing, the trucks would start back north with six hundred pounds of fish. Back at Bahía, the gulls and pelicans cleaned up the mess, and the locals counted their fresh pesos.

But three teachers from small California colleges also came down the blacktop to Bahía. Instead of a freezer, Lane Mc-Donald, José Mercadé, and Rafe Payne brought college students. For José, the new road made it easier to focus his prodigious energies on field studies — in botany and marine biology — for all ages. For Rafe Payne and Lane McDonald, the hardtop to Bahía made it easy to try something they had talked about for some time, namely, counting fin whales, taking photographs to identify and keep a record of individuals, and offering a summer class to anyone who wanted to do the same.

"We designed a one-page wildlife guide," Rafe remembers, "and a fill-in-the-blanks questionnaire for fishermen: Where did you see whales? What were they doing? Time of day? Anything unusual? But we needed a central location where we could distribute the papers." Rafe stands on the sidewalk separating the square from a rock road.

"We asked the *delegado* for permission to set up a sort of a billboard here in the city park. The billboard would have a supply of questionnaires in a little box and a slot where people could return them." The idea was hatched in total faith that if you make questions freely available, the public will come of its own volition and try to find the answers. "It might have brought in some useful information, but we never got it put up."

Rafe smiles at what has been added to this part of town.

"The paintings are new," he says.

Beyond the square with its sidewalks and whitewashed walls, behind the town hall with its policeman leaning against the white stucco talking to a friend on the bench, slightly up the hill toward a scattering of small houses, is a concrete-block building. Upon its sand-colored east wall are *pinturas* that I recognize instantly. On the left is a silhouette of a man; on the right, a deer, its legs in the stiff positions of rigor mortis, its mouth slightly agape. Both figures are replicas of prehistoric, Great Mural–style Baja California rock-face paintings and, like the originals, are larger than life. Only one kind of building would have these sorts of pictures on it.

Here, in a town with no water purification or public sewer systems, where the electricity comes on at ten in the morning and goes off at ten in the evening, stands a museum. The sight brings back memories of a powerful learning experience. Once, as a result of an unexpected resignation, I found myself in the position of interim director of the University of Nebraska State Museum, a century-old institution housing millions of research specimens, ranging from intracellular parasites to meteorites and mammoth skulls. The museum operated in five buildings; its public displays attracted more visitors than any of the university's wonders except the nationally ranked football team. When I was appointed, I promptly checked out a set of keys and asked a staff member to take me on a tour. We started in the exhibits shop and ended in the dinosaur gallery. We stepped over art students drawing skeletons and walked through crowds of small children pulling their mothers from room to room.

I had always been fascinated with museums, but this administrative assignment opened my eyes to what actually happens inside them. I saw not only the scientific efforts but also the artistic ones that went into the preparation of exhibits. I was able to roam the research collections at will, watching over curators' shoulders as they handled irreplaceable specimens, some borrowed from other museums, others being readied for loan. Then, in the great galleries, I heard children's voices, as excited as those of crusty old paleontologists with a rare fossil jawbone. Day after day people from all over the world stood before the skeletons, reconstructions, rocks, and aboriginal artifacts. Confronted by the evidence of what the universe is really like, average citizens entered the mental and physical world of scientists.

Inside a museum, objects stare us in the face. And although the specimens speak to us indirectly, they nevertheless speak clearly: Might does not guarantee survival; if it did, we would still have living dinosaurs instead of compressed-air-driven models. Animals that occupied the earth hundreds of millions of years ago are hauntingly familiar; thus we easily recognize a certain fossil as a starfish although the label reads "Devonian." Life in a new environment demands adaptation; reptiles and mammals both colonized the sea, and the oceans shaped them into porpoiselike creatures as surely as it carved the mind of Coleridge's ancient mariner out of Cockney cultural stock. The human is an extraordinarily spiritual, although not necessarily Christian, species; painted wooden deities helped inspire behavior we would interpret as moral and ethical, even on a city street today. These are the kinds of lessons that museums teach.

"Where does a museum come from in a town like this?" I wonder. Standing in front of the museum in Bahía, I remembered the constant struggle for money, the halls of damaged specimens begging for climate control, the hours at budget hearings, and a traffic jam of school buses discharging their curious hoards at our doors. A museum in Bahía de los Ángeles must be the product of indescribable idealism coupled with extreme resourcefulness.

"It's mainly the work of Carolina Espinoza," Rafe answers, still staring at the new wall paintings.

"One woman built it?"

"She's mostly responsible for what you see now, but in the very beginning, way back, personally, I think the whale incident had a lot to do with it. Up to that point, I'm not sure the town was ready for it."

I wondered how an animal could get a town ready for a museum.

"Well, at about the same time some of us were talking about a billboard and a questionnaire, there was a big fishing tournament down here. Every three years or so a sport fishing group called the Vagabundos would all come to Bahía. They'd have every kind of boat imaginable. In one afternoon, all the gasoline in town would be gone.

"That was the summer a group of students were staying on Piojo Island, that flat island farthest out in the bay. There are beautiful cliffs on the east side of that island. You can sit up there and watch whales. They had walkie-talkies, so they could radio if they needed any stuff. They camped in a cave, along the side of the island. They'd go out at six in the morning and start watching whales. They were keeping track of a mother fin whale and her calf."

A man named Bob Graham and his daughter Cynthia also saw this pair of whales, but from a different perspective. As always, the morning dawned red over the islands. The bay was calm, and shadows darkened the rocky western slope of Isla Cabeza de Caballo. Six miles across the water to the north, a low-lying finger of sand — Punta La Gringa, the Lady Tourist — lay washed in early sunlight. On the water rested nearly three hundred boats, from seventeen-foot ski rigs more at home on an impoundment lake in Kansas than in the Sea of Cortés to Skipjacks and Makos — sport fishing icons — outriggers bristling. The triennial Bahía de los Ángeles fishing tournament was under way.

Bob Graham fired up the engines of his twenty-four-foot Skipjack, *Sundance*, felt the gurgling power pulsing under his feet, and smiled at his daughter Cynthia, his "fishing buddy," relaxing in back. He guided the big boat through traffic, noting the various rocky islands, some with white caps of guano, the deepening blue of the water, and tasting the misty spray that settled on his windshield. Three or four miles out, sonar pinging the bottom, they started trolling through the reddish plankton for yellowtail. The radio crackled into life. Five miles to the south, a friend in an identical boat was getting no action and had decided to try out his new props. When the other boat came alongside, Graham pulled his lines and joined his friend. The pair of Skipjacks picked up speed, surging north through the open waters beyond Isla Piojo and toward a date with disaster.

The fin whale, *Balaenoptera physalus,* was first described by Linnaeus in the tenth edition of his *Systema Naturae,* the 1758 publication that established the methods now generally used for naming animals. Specimens may grow to eighty feet long and weigh over sixty tons. Great racks of yard-long baleen hang in rows from either side of the upper jaw. The baleen itself is composed of hundreds of flattened, gently curved pieces with a horny fingernaillike texture and feathered-out ends. This apparatus forms a massive sieve. The whale gulps in ocean water and strains organisms such as krill, sardines, and squid from it. The small prey are eventually transformed, through enzyme-driven chemical reactions, into a gargantuan mass of bone and muscle.

Half a million fin whales have been killed since the turn of the century; they were once the most numerous of their family, a group that includes the minke, Bryde's, and the humpback, as well as the blue whale, the largest living organism known ever to exist on earth, dwarfing even the dinosaurs. At birth, fin whale calves are over twenty feet long and weigh four tons. They are nursed on milk the consistency of cottage cheese for six months, nearly doubling in length during that time.

And in the azure waters off Isla Piojo, studied by college students, photographed so she could be individually identified in years hence, a mother fin whale glided below the light rays penetrating the bay, watched her calf at play, and sensed, in a way we can only guess, the two boats speeding toward her at thirty knots.

Cynthia Graham, age sixteen, was standing on the bridge of the *Sundance,* watching the water rush by on the starboard side, when the boat passed over a dark shape. Her first thought was one of relief — thank God we missed it. Bob thought they had missed a shark; when you hit one you hear a thump, and they had heard nothing but the engines and seen nothing more. Seconds later, as Bob Graham remembers it:

"She came straight out of the water, two-thirds, maybe three-fourths, of her body, and laid it across the bow where my daughter usually sits to sunbathe. We went from thirty knots to zero, a dead stop. She pushed us under to the gunwales. A Skipjack's bridge is nine and a half feet off the water." He pauses. "Her eye was even with mine, looking at me. She split the upper deck; it's three-quarter-inch fiberglass. She left fifty pounds of loose flesh on the bow. If anyone had been on the front deck, they'd have been killed. We took the boat into Don Juan Cove." Bob Graham finishes his story with a scene that is very familiar to me, if not in detail, then in kind:

"There was a marine biologist who came paddling over in his kayak. He was more worried about the whale than he was about us."

Rafe Payne was not that "marine biologist," but he remembers the same morning:

"The timing was so incredible. She timed her breach so that she landed right on the bow. Could be that she was startled, but since the boat cut between her and the calf, more likely it was a purposeful breach. She stopped the boat instantly, pushed it right down to the water line." I can tell by the look on his face that he is reconstructing this event in his mind; the speed and agility displayed by an animal the size of a fin whale leaves him in silent wonder for a few moments.

"Anything like that happens, it goes through town very quickly. There are five older families here: The Smiths and the Daggetts are the oldest. The Diazes are written up in just almost everything you read about Bahía. The Ocañas own the field station building; Arnulfo came over from the mainland to work the mine. The Verdugos had a ranch down by Las Animas but moved up here when the water gave out. They would all be concerned about anything, like a whale incident and a damaged boat, that might put a bad name on sport fishing in Bahía. The town seemed very interested in doing something."

Numerous whale encounters have contributed to the local awareness of nature. In one instance a gray whale washed up below Cerro los Ángelitos, near the south end of Bahía de los Ángeles. Over the course of several months, students from Glendale College dissected it, brought the bones to town, and buried them. Eventually the skeleton was dug up and taken to the museum. A man named Bernie Tershey also found a dead fin whale floating and towed it to an island where he anchored it, hoping the skeleton could eventually be used as an exhibit. Although a tourist took a chain saw to the skull and made off with the jaw, the rest of the skeleton was eventually taken to Bahía and laid out near the town hall, much to the delight of visiting biologists. Carolina Espinoza eventually retrieved the jaw. During the 1980s whale skeletons thus began changing from curiosities into assets.

"The naturalists who'd been working down here had collected a massive amount of information from various students' projects, bird lists, plant work, and so forth," Rafe continues. "Carolina herself was originally a marine biology student who came here on vacation, married Raul, and stayed. Various people had accumulated good collections of shells and plants, all of it identified, with locations. Carolina had a collection of historical artifacts. So Carolina, because she speaks Spanish so well, and Raul, who was one of the fishing co-op officers, and José, the three of them went to the city fathers and asked for a place to set up the skeletons. They thought about pouring a slab, putting a *cabaña* or a sheet of fiberglass over it. José greatly helped the American effort; he has an incredible amount of energy. The city donated the property behind city hall. Actually it had been a dump. Carolina and José started collecting funds, a little here and there. It was all done by trust and handshake and verbal agreement."

Today Carolina Espinoza sits behind a wooden counter just inside the door of her museum, selling T-shirts. The original whale design was drawn by one of Lane McDonald's students. Nowadays you can also buy T-shirts printed from real fish coated with silk screen ink. Dead fish don't last forever, so the number of good impressions you can get from a carcass is limited. Each fish must be painstakingly inked and pressed; the art form in called *gyotaku* in Japanese and is sometimes used by Oriental fishermen to record a catch. I buy all the extra large T-shirts she has in stock.

"We generally support the museum from sales — jewelry, shells, mostly T-shirts," says Carolina. "But we've had an enormous amount of help. This museum has been built largely by volunteers."

Visitors wander in from the native plant garden, whose specimens — including a *cirio,* the strange limbless tree of the Central Desert — were transplanted and labeled by volunteers. One year a group of people from the San Diego Wild Animal Park installed a drip system to provide some water. West of the building is a partial reconstruction of a mine shaft, with large timbers arranged to look like a tunnel entrance. An ore car sits nearby on a few feet of narrow-gauge railway, and beside it stands a giant engine, its frozen worm gears and right-angle belt drives polished by curious hands. But the most significant artifacts I see are inside the building. Rows of metal folding chairs in a room filled with mollusc shells, arrowheads, and rock samples mean only one thing to a teacher: education.

"Five years ago a museum was a foreign concept," says Carolina, "and the older people still tend to think of it as a *gringo* activity." But the look on her face is the same one I've seen on dozens of museum staff members across the United States, who know exactly where their future — and perhaps that of the planet — lies. "The teenagers have started to bring things in — old coins, crystals, a fox skull, mining tools. Then they see what's here. The boys will be saying to one another, 'Look at this! Look at this!' I think they're beginning to get a sense of history, of all the plants and animals in the region."

A Mexican woman and her two children stop by for a chat. An American walks in and gazes up at the gray whale skeleton now hanging from the ceiling. After thirty years in the business, I can usually spot field biologists on the horizon. I introduce myself, and we spend a few minutes reinforcing each other's values. Denny Hahn is from the Richardson Nature Center in Minneapolis. He is on his way to Guerrero Negro, then La Paz, from where he'll take the ferry to the mainland. He plans to be traveling for five months.

"I remember the stones," says Denny. "I came down here with an adult nature tour in 1986, and we ended up moving stones out of this place so they could put in the floor."

"The local soccer team helped shovel the trenches for the foundation," adds Carolina. "They didn't even know what a museum was." She hands out brooms. The racks of baleen still need to be hung in the skeleton's mouth, but they are filled with dirt from having sat outside at Antonio's turtle tanks for the years it takes a whale to decay and bleach into a set of white bones. For the next two hours, college students will clean baleen, then climb ladders to wire the whole rack in place. I ask about a list of donors of both talent and money.

Carolina opens her record book. The first entry is two hundred dollars from José. He wrote a letter asking for donations. His targets were the Americans who leased property along the beach. The Ocañas donated mining apparatus; a retired American miner helped with the mine-shaft reconstruction. Jorje Arce hauled the concrete blocks from Ensenada to Bahía, where students unloaded them on a day of one-hundred-and-twenty-degree heat. Raul, with Oscar from the "road crew," painted the murals, reenacting on the Museo de Naturaleza y Cultura's east wall what Baja California residents had done maybe a thousand years earlier on high, sheer rock faces. As Carolina turns the pages, the record becomes long and complicated, the accounting more businesslike.

"There's no way to thank them all, to recognize everything they've done," says Carolina. She reads a sampling of entries: students from Glendale College, the University of California at Davis, San Diego State, Biola, Nebraska Wesleyan; people from the School for Field Studies, Wild Animal Park in Escondido, Rancho Santa Ana, the Connecticut Cetacean Society, the Sonoran Desert Museum; a woman who donated forty years' worth of shells, all with exact dates and localities. And the seven students from Ensenada who came down for the sole purpose of putting the whale skeleton together and hanging it from the ceiling. Now high on a ladder, Rafe's students struggle to get the heavy baleen wired in place. The last building I was in with a fully articulated whale skeleton hanging from the ceiling was the Museum of Comparative Zoology at Harvard.

Months after our visit I find a clipping from the San Diego County *Blade-Tribune,* a short feature by Deon Holt, buried in the giant stack of photocopied material Rafe has sent me. In this story Carolina remembers a day when she visited a dump site and discovered some mining artifacts, which she recognized as those collected by an American couple during their thirty years' residence in Bahía. The pair had recently rented their house, and the tenants had thrown out what they considered trash. The items were a jolt to Carolina; lying in the dump, they demonstrated how easily a society can lose a part of its history by discarding physical evidence of the past.

Sitting late at night, reading about Carolina in the dump, trying to imagine her out among those piles of broken glass, rusted cans, scallop shells, and American plastics, I remember a phone call I received from my immediate superior a week after I'd become interim director of the University of Nebraska State Museum. The university had been asked to suggest programs that could be cut from the budget. Both the museum and the Sheldon Art Gallery had been put on the list. Someone had actually written the name and account number of a major museum and of an equally distinguished art gallery upon a form and given the paper to a legislative assistant, whereupon over a century's worth of cultural, paleontological, biological, and geological collections, and an equally long record of human vision as a reflection of its society, became expendable.

I complained. I was told that if my staff had three million dollars' worth of grant money, the museum would not be in jeopardy. I walked back through the art gallery — a panorama of important American Expressionists on the walls — to my own building, a giant parade of fully articulated mammoth and mastodont skeletons still holding the rapt attention of hundreds of elementary school children. The telephone rang. The mother of a child who loved Elephant Hall had just heard the news.

Before the year was out, she and others like her put together a coalition of teachers, parents, and students that descended upon the state legislature like a pack of hungry bankers. Their effort succeeded. But when the budget memo had first crossed my desk, I had felt like someone who had gone to the dump and found his culture, his knowledge of the natural world, tossed out by new tenants. Yes, I could easily see how an encounter with real specimens lying in the trash, the same tools held by human hands and pounded into the Santa Marta Mountain rock in search of gold before she was born, might unleash Carolina's energies and sustain them for years.

So far Carolina's museum has remained free of the trappings of an urban society. It shines, bare, unpretentious, yet effective, as do other things on the desert. On any day any person can take a field trip there, live the lives of miners, anthropologists, zoologists, historians, within the single display room of this concrete-block building, using specimens that in most cases they are allowed to touch. A child can repeat at will what I have waited decades to do: go exploring in a strange land, maybe even a country of the imagination, in order to relearn something about the earth that supports us.

12

Ordovician Earrings

Paleontologists tell us that our planet has experienced several massive extinctions; in each the diversity of life was greatly diminished. The two most striking extinctions occurred two hundred and thirty million years ago, at the end of the Permian period, when, some scientists estimate, ninety percent of all species died out, and then seventy million years ago, at the closing of the Cretaceous, when the dinosaurs disappeared. We see each of these events as a blink in the fossil record, but they probably occurred over centuries, if not millennia. A third truly major reduction in global diversity is taking place as you read this paragraph. Tropical forests are being cleared for short-term agricultural use at the rate of about a hundred acres a minute. Seventy percent of the genetic information that spells "life on earth" is found in these forests. By the time you finish this chapter, a square mile will be gone forever. A hundred million years from now, biologists studying mass extinctions may reflect on the twentieth century A.D. and marvel at the thousands of species that evolved from the cockroach, rat, starling, and English sparrow gene pools.

Our present array of Baja California animals, as wondrous as it is, results from elaboration on a relatively few themes left over after perhaps dozens of others vanished. Many potential species that could have evolved from Cretaceous ancestors are gone, in the same sense that all commitments destroy options. My choice to become a parasitologist, made in the heady excitement of youth surrounded by articulate, thoughtful people, dealt a mortal blow to my chances of becoming a polychaete taxonomist. The pressures of surviving on the faculty of a major university, coupled with the parade of students who demanded attention and rewarded me with careers of their own, narrowed my intellectual focus day by day. My return to the seashore at the age of fifty-two reminds me, as a trip to the museum does, that healthy diversity — be it among plants and animals or among scientists who study them — is a product of choice and rejection. You always wonder what might have transpired had you made different choices and different rejections. But you know that the challenges of survival, even as a teacher, would still have had to be met.

Every naturalist knows that animal life has been solving the same problems over and over since the fossil record began, namely, how to cope with temperature variation, find water, move, reduce the chances of being eaten, and produce fertile offspring, among other items in the long list of feats a successful species must accomplish. Walking on the beach at sunrise, kicking shells, reviewing my reasons for collecting some, leaving others, I conclude that on the grandest scale, the puzzle that life faces is not one of choosing among many options — that choice has been made for it in the past mass extinctions — but of generating diversity out of a constrained set of raw materials. This paradoxical character of evolutionary history — extreme conservation coupled with apparent profusion of type — is evident from even a cursory study of molluscs. Those species in the Pacific Ocean and the Gulf of California are as good as any for such a purpose.

Members of the bivalve genus *Chama* live attached to hard substrates, including rocks and sometimes even one another; the shells are typically ornamented with scales that project out in layers roughly parallel to the concentric growth lines. The differences among *Chama* species are sometimes subtle, but they all represent elaborations on a theme: diversity built upon uniformity. In at least one species, from the South Pacific, the flanges are drawn out into long, almost tubular, spines with branching ends. Comparison of *Chama* species from all over the world reveals enough variation in scale structure — from leaflike to spiny — that simply by holding, feeling, and seeing their shells, one is able to understand how one characteristic might be only a modified version of another.

In this manner the study of clams easily evolves into a general lesson instead of a specific one. By considering the shell as a metaphor rather than a biological specimen, we learn how to construct a seemingly unique and complex trait from another trait that on the surface appears quite different (pun intended!) but that possesses the fundamental elements of the first. When viewed alone, a scale seems nothing like a spine. But when we see a shell that has raised and partly rolled ridges, we make the obvious connection between the two features: a spine is nothing more than an elongated and rolled-up scale. By the same means, we can construct histories of change and divergence. These histories may not be the same ones scientists recover using molecular and statistical methods, but as purely mental exercises, they are equally instructive. The bivalves in this example — *Chama* species — are not particularly rare or unusual. They have lived in the

Gulf of California since the Upper Pliocene; collectors call them "jewel boxes."

Species of the clam genus *Chione* live buried in the intertidal gravel among slivers of dark stones worn smooth from their dragging and pounding by waves. Natives and tourists alike dig for *Chione*. The beach gravel north of Punta La Gringa has an almost sensual feel as I sift through spadeful after spadeful, pausing to study individual rocks and putting a few in my pocket. The mostly gray, oblong, flattened pebbles reflect the geological jigsaw that surrounds me: an extinct river or tide channel at my back, an alluvial finger, tipped by gneiss outcrops, pointing toward the south and, a few yards to the west, the broken, twisted face of truly ancient, maybe even Paleozoic, rock laid bare along a fault line. Beyond a low cliff the gulf pounds against a conglomerate shore; across the channel, Smith Island's mixture of basalt, andesite, and metamorphic sediments displays subtly shifting colors, seemingly oblivious of the wind. My companions are scattered in small groups, down on their knees, digging with their hands. They find just enough *Chione* to keep them looking for more.

Back at the field station the little clams are thrown into boiling water to cook until their shells gape. We use spoons to scrape out the foot, visceral mass, and mantle, which we then toss into a pot; periodically I toss one into my mouth instead of the pot; they are delicious even without the rest of the chowder. But there's not much protein in a single clam; a gallon bucket of *Chione* reduces to tidbits on the stove. Then Rafe pours in spices, a secret recipe for stew over rice. As I gorge, I wonder what animals ate *Chione* from the western shores of the Sea of Cortés before humans evolved. *Chione californiensis* has lived at Bahía de los Ángeles since the middle Pliocene.

The next day, sitting on the VSFS patio, I while away an afternoon watching gulls carry bivalves up into the air and drop them on the rocks. Having made *Chione* stew the night before, I suddenly take a rather personal interest in this behavior. Gulls may have been dropping clams, cracking the shells, and eating the soft parts for as long as there have been gulls. Is clam dropping learned or instinctive? If learned, it is a cultural trait that has been passed down by birds generation after generation. Gulls have been on earth for about six million years, and it's conceivable that they acquired this behavior from their ancestors. Such a history would make the wood rats' eight-thousand-year habit of using cholla joints for nests a rather recent, almost modern, innovation.

Glen joins me on the patio, watches the seabirds for a few minutes, and tells me a story he has heard about gulls putting clams on the road, then waiting for cars to smash them. From the tone of his voice, I sense that he doesn't necessarily believe this tale. I'm skeptical too, not only about the source of information, but especially about the birds' supposed intent. In a scientist's view of the universe, a gull's behavior is explained as being directed by its desired ends only after all other explanations for that behavior have been rigorously excluded by research.

However, I once heard a behaviorist speak of "cultural transmission" — the teaching of an acquired character — in fish, namely group-specific courtship rituals among sticklebacks. Although she stopped far short of claiming purpose in their actions, her field data nevertheless showed that sticklebacks learned from one another in nature. School is formalized cultural transmission. If a gull learns to drop clams by trial and error, then learns to distinguish rocks from sand as targets of differing efficacy, then the bird has solved a practical problem in the management of food resources. But if gulls learn this behavior from other gulls, then they have "been to school." And if the dropping of bivalves "in order to break the shells" is an instance of cultural transmission, then the feeding behavior of gulls also reveals the human arrogance by which other species are denied certain intellectual capacities, especially the very ones behind our development of technology. But the limitations of birds are, after all, real: No gull makes a chowder like Raphael Payne's!

Members of the genus *Ostrea* are easily recognized as oysters by anyone who has ever eaten in a seafood restaurant. Their heavy, irregular, chalky, six- or eight-inch shells can be dug from a clay lens on the side of a road cut near San Ignacio. Overlying this crumbly formation is a thick layer of red lava, weathered into boulder-sized chunks. Cardons rise up majestically through the basalt; turkey vultures rest on the tips of scarred branches, warming their wings in the January dawn. Below the exposed oysters, in the tangle of weeds, cans, bottles, lies a pile of feces, a dirty disposable diaper, and a dead dog. I step over the dog and balance against the road cut wall, scraping at one fossil shell with a piece of another. A vermilion flycatcher flits into an elephant tree, then disappears over a chain link fence. For thousands of centuries only the site, not the form, of oyster life has changed. A bed that was maybe a hundred feet below the ocean surface now lies halfway up a high ridge. Bivalves feed by trapping microscopic particles on their gills, which hang in sheets between the shell and the body; *Ostrea* species have filtered diatoms and other one-celled organisms from the Baja California waters since the lower Pliocene.

If *Chama* demonstrates the generation of diversity from superficial traits — spines from flanges — and if *Chione* chowder leads to a discussion of food preparation by gulls and biologists, then oysters suffice for a study of extreme variability around a mysterious core pattern, that is, the elusiveness of central theme. With oysters we see the same general problems of cognition that we did with cacti. The "official" species descriptions could not be more frustrating to a rookie; because they are scientific, the cold words for structure are easily assumed to be precise as well. The vocabulary of oyster taxonomy cannot be easily acquired without a series of shells in hand and some guidance — the right book or teacher — nearby. In *Ostrea* the prodissoconch hinge is long, the muscle scar is central and not colored, and lateral shell margins can be finely crenulated or finely denticulate, depending on the species.

But you have to be an "expert," initiated into the cult of those who see things others cannot, to pick these fixed features out of a collection of individual specimens. Had our own species been on earth since the early Pliocene, as oysters have, we could have worked at training ourselves to do such a task for seven million years. Linnaeus named *Ostrea edulis,* a European species, in 1758. Although for the next century most oyster species were included in *Ostrea,* some have since been assigned to other genera, based on their hinges and scar color. Thus someone eventually learned to solve the cognitive puzzles, to recognize certain consistent patterns amid a forest of variable traits.

As a group, the bivalves have been extraordinarily successful for a very long time, well back into the Paleozoic era. But their feeding mechanism — use of gill cilia to filter tiny particles out of the water — places limits on their ability to occupy certain environments and on their role in animal communities. For example, there are no truly terrestrial clams, nor are there any predatory ones. There are, however, bivalve species that swim, burrow into mud, wood, or stone, get pounded by heavy surf and exposed to the air for long periods during low tide, and live in the ocean, shallow estuaries, abyssal seas, and freshwater lakes, streams, and rivers. Bivalves occur in soft muds and gravels and on rocks; they attach to the latter by protein strands or shell-like secretions. Characteristics that might seem to us like formidable limitations — filter feeding using gills, soft body, and seemingly limited ability to move — have hardly stopped the bivalves from evolving into an amazing diversity of types.

In the chapter "Keeper of the Keys," I talked about the liberating effects of extreme constraint in the case of writing assignments given to college students. Perhaps this is a good place to expand on another such instance. I asked two hundred freshmen in a zoology class to write five three-page papers about a specimen from the invertebrate paleontology gallery of a museum. One of these papers was to be a piece of fiction, a story that would inspire Maria — the eight-year-old child of migrant farm workers — to want to become a marine biologist. At least three-fourths of my students, including the women, wrote action adventure stories involving the rescue of a female invertebrate from a life-threatening situation by a male invertebrate of their chosen species.

I sat in my living room chair through the late night hours, reading page after page, wondering what had gone through the minds of these students when they started their stories. In the end I realized that the tales were only a reflection of what a society was telling itself about the ways of the world through popular literature — including films, news emphasis, and television, in addition to books. I concluded that storytelling, among the most powerful of art forms, was a far more important skill to acquire than that of writing contracts, treating physical illness, or managing large corporations.

In our science courses, however, we spend an enormous amount of time teaching students to solve small problems and do analyses, when we probably should be teaching them to influence someone else. Maybe by doing the latter we'd eventually produce a political leader who would be comfortable addressing scientific problems in an objective way.

The students whose field trips to Baja California I had joined as a tagalong spent many hours on a series of assignments. They had to keep a journal, take quizzes, read, formally discuss their thoughts and observations, and eventually write papers. Their biological backgrounds ranged from fairly extensive to almost nil. Teri Trendler, the young woman who held the sick pelican while I painted its picture, worked with animals at Sea World; Tony Buhr, one of Glen's students from Nebraska Wesleyan, was a football player who would eventually go to graduate school to study molecular biology; and Bill Moser, from my own advanced classes at the University of Nebraska, was already a leech expert (at least compared to the rest of us!) by the time he was a junior in college. At the other extreme were students from conservative religious schools who were taking the trip to fulfill their science requirement. Although this last group displayed a keen business sense and excellent writing and speaking skills, few if any had ever touched wild plants or animals, much less studied them.

One of the Biola students, Cindy Spiva, was a serious photographer, a highly artistic, well-read, deep-thinking, insightful, and mature person who wanted to eventually become a writer. In her uncompromising individuality, she reminded me of my own daughter, also named Cindy, who was just as determined to make her way in the world by the use of her creative talents. I could see among my companions almost a full range of the kinds of people who would do the business and direct the thinking, as well as the subsequent actions, of my nation. Like all teachers, I thought of these students as my intellectual children, a feeling strengthened considerably by the presence of Cindy Spiva. As the days passed, I found myself thinking more and more about their futures, the patterns of their lives, the way in which my generation, through its science and its storytelling, shaped those patterns, and what my obligations were in this matter of maintaining a civilized society in a world of rapidly diminishing resources. That is, what should I teach?

The bivalves we handled reminded me of the timelessness of certain problems and of the ephemerality and restricted scope of others. I could pick up a clam and see in it not only a recipe for stew but also a shell pattern that had been present on earth for many millions of years. I could dig out an oyster fossil and hold not only a valuable specimen but, for me, a reminder of how difficult it is to find a common theme, a common ground, among exceedingly diverse objects. And in these apparently different views of shells, I saw decisions to be made in my remaining time on earth: Do I teach my children to grow oysters for sale or to use them in a story that would make eight-year-old Maria become a marine biologist? At the heart of this dilemma is the difference between science and technology, or rather the misperception that one *is* the other.

Science is simply exploration of the natural world. Science makes discoveries, while technology solves practical problems. Science, not unlike literature and philosophy, generates concepts, ideas, and world views; technology makes products for sale. Science is sustained by curiosity, technology by money and political power. Science *(S)* borrows unashamedly and often unconcernedly from technology *(T);* technology is parasitic upon science: If S dies, then T dies; T sucks resources from $S;$ the sequential development of T is inextricably linked to the environmental cues provided by $S;$ the great bulk of S depends on a relatively common and constrained set of $T,$ while the truly massive accumulations of technology are found in only a few sciences. Parasite populations, for example, hookworms in humans, obey these last two numerical rules —

most people don't have them, while a few people have a lot. Businesses, and academic institutions run in a businesslike manner, are generally incapable of distinguishing between *S* and *T*. Thus they merge the two. The results of this fusion are well summarized by Norman Mailer in *Cannibals and Christians:*

> Beautiful women, literary people, social planners, editorial writers, presidents, politicians, and a sprinkling of illiterates do not know that science is most exact in those regions where it has progressed into the secrets of the universe about as far as the precision and exactitude of English spelling has advanced us into the secret lore of meaning. Which is to say: a distance. But not a great distance. Where science is exact, it is vastly insignificant; where it is significant, it is open-ended, not certain, prey to reasoning by analogy, torn by debate, sustained by darkest mystery, and when all is said, about as scientific as literary criticism.

Mailer implies that scientists must teach the general public to distinguish between machinery and concepts and to look across vast reaches of time and space, through the proximal wilderness of a complex society and into the ultimate scheme of things. It was for this last reason, then, that I bought our daughter a pair of little ark shell earrings. I had found the Gulf of California bivalves a rich source of ideas, a stimulus for both serious biology and storytelling, and was convinced she would too. A colorful array of handmade jewelry hung on a board in the gift shop of the Museo de Bahía de los Ángeles. Most of the pieces were made from limpet shells; their oval shape, off-turquoise lining, and rough exteriors are symbols for a cup of beauty held by gnarled hands. But the little arks were, like our daughter, a rare find among the wandering millions scattered on various beaches.

Arks, like oysters, are bivalve molluscs. Their fossil ancestors are uncovered in Ordovician deposits four hundred and fifty million years old, and living arks are found in many places in the world today, including the Gulf of California. Bivalves are classified and identified in part by their hinge teeth. Ark shells have "taxodont" teeth — a long row of short parallel ridges and grooves at right angles to the hinge line. This general tooth arrangement is typical of the earliest bivalves; the majority of more recent clams have very different kinds of teeth. Our daughter Cindy could stick a wire loop through the hole in her ear and walk around dangling a life pattern that has survived for nearly half a billion years. I reasoned that such jewelry, and its symbolism, might help her survive another New England winter.

The earrings were a perfectly matched pair, right and left valves. I told her how to distinguish right from left, which brief biology lesson gave her the option of hanging left valve from right ear, or vice versa, depending on the political statement she wanted to make. So if she needed assurance that a pattern of existence at right angles to the major articulations of society could survive the massive Mesozoic extinctions, all she had to do was look at her earrings. And if she was in the dark when she needed this reassurance, she could reach up and touch them. Taxodont teeth are as easily read with the fingers as Braille.

Pattern in living organisms consists of repeated, and thus predictable, structures and events, ranging from single small bones to the fishing behavior of boobies. At its most fundamental level, "knowledge" is simply the ability to recognize a pattern and put a word — a name — on it. The name is usually one that someone else has assigned to the form we observe. But when we are the first to recognize a particular pattern, we get to choose the name. And if our choice is shown to be the first name used to refer to a particular phenomenon, we are said to have "made a discovery."

We often equate knowledge of patterns with the ability to

increase the "bottom line." In academia we claim that if you learn to predict an event when presented with information, then people will pay you some money to use your acquired skills. But so many designs have been present on earth for so many eons that learning how to complete a sequence started by another (predict an outcome from an occurrence) begins to seem like a trivial exercise. Certain similar shapes have repeatedly evolved from stocks that either were unrelated genetically or were separated by astronomical lengths of time.

The bivalve form itself is an excellent case in point. We have bivalve trilobites, molluscs, and brachiopods and two major groups of unrelated bivalved crustaceans. Wings are another illustration: Insects, reptiles, birds, and mammals all acquired wings independently. Penguins "fly" through the water, as do manta rays and some gastropods, the latter demonstrating that flight motions are not the exclusive property of insects and vertebrates. The arcane literature of classical zoology contains many additional, although not as readily appreciated, examples of convergence and parallelism in structure. Long-lived and independently repeated designs can be thought of as proven solutions to fundamental problems. But we live with fundamental problems that seem to have defied solution: runaway population growth, violent conflict between cultures, institutionalized sexism and racism. Ancient tooth patterns on clam shells make me wonder whether the solutions have been lying around undiscovered for eons, to be found if we just spent enough time on beaches.

The variety of bivalves at my feet is hardly more diverse than what I would have found walking Paleozoic shores. In addition to arks, a number of forms not easily distinguishable from living species, at first glance of an untrained eye, must have littered those primeval coasts. *Similodonta* — fossils from the Ordovician and Silurian — show growth rings on their outer surfaces — a record of years lost in the dawn of planetary history — and an offset umbo (the "beak" or first part of the shell formed). If I found this fossil among the intertidal bits and pieces today, I would probably call it a *Chione.* Then I'd turn it over and look at the teeth. Suddenly the strange stonelike texture of the specimen would be explained; I would be holding not the remnants of last night's meal, but something that disappeared three hundred million years ago. My first impressions would have been wrong; careful study would reveal the truth. *Nuculoidea,* also dead, gone before the dinosaurs came, shows flared posterior edges on its valves, an asymmetry that is repeated by dozens, if not hundreds, of living bivalves. *Paleoneilo* lies embedded in rock, spread as if washed up, inside down, with the valves still attached by their hinge ligament. Funny, that picture of an Ordovician clam looks just like my photograph of a Pismo on the sand at San Quintín.

I have a sense that this long persistence of certain life shapes subconsciously reminded me of our daughter, which in turn is why I grabbed the ark shell earrings so quickly. She'd decided to be a writer, and by the tender age of twenty-seven had generated a couple of requisite first novels, short stories, and probably a notebook full of poetry, along with a real writer's burgeoning supply of rejection slips. Her plans carried her from the fertile gardens of Berkeley, the stages of various rock band gigs, the physical labor of menial outdoor jobs, back to the Central Plains for the express purpose of "experiencing the Nebraska winter as a groundskeeper," and finally to Boston for graduate work.

I walked the sand at El Coyote, picked shells, and enjoyed the fruits of my mental labor; I had learned enough during the past quarter-century to be able to recognize patterns and put names on them in an exotic setting. That is, I had seen these shells before. But why did my intellectual stroll through molluscan history remind me of Cindy and stimulate me to buy her some Ordovician earrings? Because in pursuit of her dreams, she opted to spend her life *making* patterns instead of recognizing them. I knew that if she kept on trying, she would eventually produce the equivalent of a new species — one more solution to the age-old problem of living successfully.

13

Guerrero Negro

⌐⌐he line separating Baja California Norte from Baja California Sur is marked by a gigantic abstract steel-beam sculpture. The line is the twenty-eighth parallel, and on it, northeast of Scammon's Lagoon, lies Guerrero Negro. Blowing sand and salt marshes provide the geological setting, the historical elements, that direct the lives of those who live in Guerrero Negro. The battered blacktop road into town is lined with an array of taco stands, grocery stores, tire repair shops, and motels, but the economy of Guerrero Negro depends mostly on salt taken from the nearby lagoon. Down the street from the salt company headquarters is a beautiful city park. In that park, under a gazebo, a young man named Eric encountered a ragtag bunch of Americans looking at birds. And it was there Eric discovered that when language failed, he could talk to strangers with his art.

Winter bird watchers in Baja California are possibly of more interest than the winter birds. Aside from the few endemic species — Heermann's gull in the gulf, the vermilion flycatcher — the winter fauna consists mainly of familiar northern and Pacific Coast breeders in dull plumage. The dowitcher that we see in late spring in Nebraska has the same body proportions but different shadings from one in the ditch along a dike road west of Guerrero Negro. But a dowitcher it turns out to be after all. In this sense the bird is similar to its watcher; a businessman in Seattle is not the same creature as the one who drives his luxury van slowly along the brutal, pockmarked roads through the salt flats, although he may occupy the same body. And the metamorphosis of the human is no less important a subject for study than the dowitcher's molt.

The bird brings the man into Mexico, and the man brings money. This joint migration happens often enough, and has happened for enough years, that twelve-year-old boys on the streets of Guerrero Negro find bird watchers to be a species no more exotic than the birds. But of all the kids in town that afternoon, only one was drawn to a knot of American college students standing in the city park, all holding binoculars to their eyes and staring intently at some object a few feet away.

Geology had brought us to the area, and architecture to the park itself. The unique physical geology of the Guerrero Negro region provides for the manufacture of salt by evaporative methods, using dikes, pools, and the sun's rays. The combination of natural land forms, tides, and radiant energy is what allows the operation. But this combination also draws tourists, for the marshes and salt flats attract massive numbers of birds — herons, sandpipers, pelicans. Some people who punish their front suspensions out on the dike roads seek rarity; they scan the flocks for an out-of-place tern. Others look for the art to be found in patterns of avocets sleeping, a flock of dunlins twisting, turning, flashing light from the underside of their wings, or a dozen snowy egrets pushing air above the dark weeds. When familiarity is displayed in rare form, it is every bit as attractive as a rarity itself.

Serious bird watchers find and remember choice spots, be

they vast marshes, secret stretches of woodland, or even, in some cases, single trees. Raphael Payne is a serious bird watcher. For three full days he slowly drove the pounding dike roads at Guerrero Negro. On each of these excursions, the combination of van window glass, binoculars, and telephoto lenses produced headache pain that made me think of experimental neurosurgery, professional boxing, and the worst hangover on record, all experienced simultaneously as I was trying to work up enough spit to swallow four aspirins. Then he stopped at a plywood shack, where we bought and ate obscene numbers of fish tacos liberally laced with *salsa,* which cleared my sinuses like a nail driven through the roof of my mouth. Then he said let's go to the city park; we always find redstarts in the city park. We had gone to as many places, as many different habitats, as we could reasonably visit in three weeks, and had not once seen a redstart. At that point every redstart on earth could have flown into the bougainvillea-covered gazebo in the Guerrero Negro city park, and I would not have cared a damn for any of them.

But sure enough, there they were, along with Costa's hummingbirds, which I found infinitely more fascinating than redstarts. Fascination is an abstraction, and although it's in quite a different realm from lava flows and elephant trees, it is nevertheless real and definable; you can take possession of fascination and use it as a resource. Standing in the park, I could not envision a situation in which redstarts could compete successfully with hummingbirds for human attention. Rafe was excited about redstarts, however; both males and females flitted quickly through the flowering vines. Like any bird watcher who has returned to a favorite place and discovered what he came for, he found his biological knowledge validated. Such confirmations are personally important when the knowledge is not something learned from a book but acquired through experience.

Then someone became aware of a Mexican boy standing among us. His eyes were wide, dark and, above all, alert, with a slight touch of fear of the place he'd been drawn into by his curiosity. His fingers worked a small piece of clay. He nodded at the gazebo and raised his eyebrows; we all understood immediately what he was asking: What are twenty Norte Americanos so captivated by that they're all staring at it through binoculars even though it's right in front of their eyes? Rafe never lowered his glasses; he focused on the redstarts and talked about them in a steady stream. But one of the students instantly answered the boy's unspoken question. She opened her bird book and showed him a picture of a Costa's hummingbird. Aha! I thought; redstarts lost the competition in another's mind, too!

A smile crossed the boy's face, and within seconds, it seemed, he'd fashioned a perfect hummingbird out of the clay. The head and tail were in a jaunty, almost feisty, attitude; I wouldn't have been surprised had the little sculpture come alive in his hand and flown away. In Berlitz-style Spanish we asked him his name.

"¿Como se llama?"

"Eric."

"¿Cuantos años tiene?" And his age.

"Doce."

Twelve. Eric was a twelve-year-old Mexican boy who carried a lump of clay. I had no idea what he'd been molding before he saw us, but I imagined it could easily have been any of the elements of his environment — palm trees, pickup trucks, a bus slowly being stripped of its wiring, loaves in the panadería, abalone shells from piles on the dikes, giant rusted beams and pulleys at the salt pier, a twin-engine airplane banking sharply to land in the Guerrero Negro wind.

I wondered why we seemed to want to know Eric's name right away, while we had never asked the old fisherman at El

Coyote. Was the difference in Eric's art? Or do grownups the world over ask kids their name and age just because other topics seem too deep, too serious, for children? Or were we thinking, subconsciously, that the clay hummingbird symbolized higher aspirations, while Kino's wooden boat represented slavery to a life of subsistence fishing? As I watched Eric work the clay, I tried to remember when I had seen another child, on the streets of any town, continuously making sculpture, and I couldn't think of a single instance.

Early exposure to art, especially the hands-on making of it, helps develop talents essential to successful work in a number of fields. We are such a visually oriented species that we constantly change words into diagrams and vice versa. We talk about "sentence structure" in our essays, put "loops" into our computer programs, and build "models" made of assertions and observations. Suddenly, after converting our own ideas into figures, we're better able to understand others' expressions, often acknowledging that understanding with the common metaphor "I see."

Geologists and architects, however, two groups that rely heavily on their ability to represent concepts graphically, also regularly do something that "pure" artists accomplish only indirectly, namely add the fourth dimension — time — to their "pictures." Knowledge of the past is crucial to the geologist's business, and predictions are equally as important to the architect's. The soil types and climates that surround us are products of global events that not only leave a record of their occurrence but also determine the economic base, and with it the culture, of a region. These conditions usually cannot be changed very much. The only alternative to living in our environment is to shield ourselves from it. But what we can do tomorrow is, to a large extent, determined by whatever edifice we have made for ourselves today.

Thus history and design are both boundary conditions for

a future. And in Guerrero Negro the boundary conditions into which Eric was born were established by wind and salt. Eric's father probably worked for the Exportadora de Sal and the boy himself, if his art didn't take him away from Guerrero Negro, might well do the same. The harvesting of sodium chloride has been practiced in many parts of the world for centuries — from the southern coasts of Spain to central Kansas — wherever geological events have produced the necessary landscape and mineral supplies. But today the goal is not simply to get sea salt from sea water, but to get pure sodium chloride in industrial quantities. The chemistry of these methods is reasonably straightforward: As water evaporates, the minerals of low solubility precipitate out first, leaving behind the more soluble ones. The water can then be transferred to another container and allowed to evaporate more so that the next least soluble materials precipitate. With successive transfers of water and evaporations, the various comounds of sodium, potassium, calcium, and magnesium can be separated.

If sodium chloride were either the least or the most soluble of ocean salts, this technique for purifying it would be exceedingly simple in practice. However, it is the next to the most soluble. Thus, in order to get it out of the ocean in relatively pure form, you must evaporate until everything but sodium and magnesium chloride precipitates, move the water, then evaporate just enough to precipitate the sodium chloride, then move the water again. As a lab exercise, this work takes more patience than brains. As an industrial process, it requires a great deal of energy to move and evaporate enormous quantities of sea water.

Out on the brine pans south and west of Guerrero Negro, high-volume pumps pull water from Scammon's Lagoon, then move it from one pool to another as the various compounds precipitate under the relentless sun. Giant bulldozers scrape the salt out of crystal beds that from a distance look like snowfields. But the enterprise is evidently worth the effort. In the middle 1980s the United States consumed more than forty million tons of salt a year, valued at nearly seven hundred million dollars, and imported almost a fourth of Mexico's entire salt production — nearly two million tons, worth over twenty-five million dollars. The Exportadora de Sal has been good to Guerrero Negro; the children are well dressed, and the library, in the park near the redstart gazebo, is an elegant building with beautiful interior woodwork.

Evaporative salt harvesting the world over requires the handling of massive amounts of one of the most common and relatively corrosive substances on earth. Unlike the old mining cars at Bahía de los Ángeles, which seem to acquire a desert varnish, the abandoned salt pier at Guerrero Negro is frozen in rust. In another setting the dismembered framework of giant beams connecting at right angles to each other could be an abstract sculpture. Packed in beat-up small cars with dirty windows, locals drive the dike roads to the lighthouse, then walk out on the beams to sit and fish and write graffiti. Gears are sealed in rust; kids step over holes in half-inch-thick steel plates; rebar writhes out of broken concrete like a colony of giant red-brown pockmarked worms. Ospreys glare down from their nests — tangles of sticks on thin, dark pillars — scream, shake their wings, then shoot streams of feces into the offshore wind. An injured cormorant backs into a washed-out crevice alongside a piling.

The old lighthouse is the tallest structure for miles, maybe even the tallest between the ocean and the mountains. Looking inland from the pier, I see nothing but low vegetation, tide channels, vast brine pans, mudflats. Six species of heron sit on a single, slightly raised spit of wet sand; great blues stand perfectly still, gazing down into the water; black- and yellow-crowned night herons hunker down in the *Salicornia;*

a reddish egret waits, toes laid gently on an old tire; a small flock of cattle egrets lifts out of the brush and battles the wind for a few hundred yards before settling along the edge of the dike road. I scan the scene with binoculars, then take my turn at the spotting scope. No matter which direction I look, I see birds; as far as the lenses take me, toward the horizon, I see gulls, brant, plovers, sandpipers of all sizes, pelicans, cormorants — sitting, sleeping, poking their bills into the mud, or flying through the shimmering reflections off distant pools.

The plain upon which Guerrero Negro rests stretches nearly a hundred miles north and south and almost half that distance east and west. The coastal lagoons contain both ocean- and wind-borne sediments. Tidal flooding, followed by evaporation, concentrates the enormous load of nutrients carried by seawater, making a fertile place for the algal growth that supports the food pyramid of protozoa, crustacea, molluscs, small fish, and seabirds. Channels course through the more stabilized dunes topped with salt grass and pickleweed; the currents are slowed by the vegetation, so particles settle out. Wind blows sand off the deserts to the east, as well as from the coastal areas to the northwest, and the dust gathers in the marsh and on the dunes. The tidal flats are thus a dynamic ecosystem; a careful examination of the lagoon system reveals it to be as protean as the clay lump in Eric's hands.

During the 1960s a scientist named Fred Phleger from the Scripps Institution of Oceanography came to Guerrero Negro, along with a number of assistants, to analyze the mechanics of coastal marsh and dune formation. From his study of bivalve shells, amoeba skeletons, tide channel currents, and prevailing winds, Phleger concluded that the lagoon was formed about seven thousand years ago, beginning with a sand barrier, when sea level was forty feet lower than it is today. As the ocean rose, the barrier continued to be built from wave-borne sediments. Although sea level has remained stable for about two thousand years, the beach has moved seaward almost a mile during that time. The shipping docks have also been moved, from the old site now used mainly by bird watchers and fishermen, to the south, where the new salt pier is closer to the main channel between the open ocean and the Laguna Ojo de Liebre.

Among Phleger's many discoveries, the distribution of microscopic skeletons is the one I find the most fascinating. Single-celled animals called foraminiferans, a kind of amoeba, build intricate, chambered tests that at first glance appear strikingly similar to molluscan shells. Foraminiferans have been on earth for several hundred million years; their skeletons are used not only as indicator fossils — revealing the age and original ecological setting of sedimentary rocks — but also as evidence of the mosaic nature of the present-day tidal flats. Phleger and his co-workers recognized distinct groupings of foraminiferan species, typical of the near-shore ocean, the inner lagoon, and the marsh itself. These amoebas occur in astronomical numbers — up to a thousand in a shot-glass-sized sample.

The processes that produce foraminiferan skeletons are as mysterious as those that produce clay hummingbirds. Pattern formation in single-celled animals is as difficult to explain as the inheritance of artistic talent. Books are filled with descriptions of gene expression; even freshman texts go into great detail about the biochemistry of RNA and polypeptide synthesis, operator and promoter genes, and the classic case of genetic control, namely the stimulation of enzyme production by bacteria supplied with milk sugar. But you will not find a paper in any journal that says *exactly* how a blob of cytoplasm is able to construct a design of incredible delicacy from calcium and silicon salts. There is plenty of literature that tells how to build a kiln, stretch a canvas, or mix pigments. But there are no instructions for making art that stands the test of time. The complete DNA sequence of the human species, once it is recorded in computers, will tell us nothing about the Cro-Magnon cave paintings, which look as contemporary as anything done in the past century.

In retrospect, it seems rather romantic to let a young Mexican boy's hummingbird bring to mind all these thoughts about patterns — the geological ones resulting from natural forces at work, the geologists' attempts to represent the rock and soil formations, the buildings that lend a town its character, the expressions of emotion, and the fine designs of one-celled animal skeletons. But in the most general sense, there was more similarity than difference between the little sculpture and the sum total of Guerrero Negro. And the brown fingers molding the clay represented, at least to me, all forces, both human and natural, that shape our world.

We offered coins for Eric's performance. He shook his head; he didn't want money. We insisted, but the well-dressed young man continued to shake his head, until at last we succeeded in forcing him to take some pesos. He had been excited at first as he made the life-sized hummer, but when we held out the coins, he became frightened and disappointed. The fragile relationship had been broken; by our offer he'd been sent into the ranks of street peddlers instead of accepted into our midst as an artist.

As quickly as it had appeared, the sculpture vanished into an amorphous dynamic lump, with only the lingering spirit, the potential to be a hummingbird, that we now knew lived in the clay. Eric's hands worked at the clay while we turned back to the gazebo. The hummers came and went, appearing suddenly, then disappearing, materializing as easily and unexpectedly as the one in Eric's hands had done, then flashing away, leaving only a red flower nodding in the winter salt breeze. I became aware, then, of a small hand holding up a new form. Eric had made a tiny bust of an American college professor bird watcher. His skilled use of a stick had even conveyed the unmistakable and correct impression that I was in rather bad need of a haircut. Amid the laughter that followed, we again offered pesos, but this time the quick headshake and stern eyes said we should have known better. He offered the clay bust. I accepted it.

We asked Eric if he drew pictures or painted. He nodded vigorously; the smile returned as he dropped to his knees and, with the same motion the fisherman at our campfire had used, smoothed a place on the ground and used a stick to sketch a tropical scene: beach, palm trees, brilliant and searing sun. He finished by writing "La Paz." Someone handed him a pencil and a notebook. He knelt with the notebook against his leg and began to draw. As he worked, I opened my own book and sketched: a drawing of a Mexican boy drawing. His picture on paper was identical to the one he'd made in the dirt, and he labeled it, as he'd done before, "La Paz." I wrote "Eric drawing in the park at Guerrero Negro" on mine, signed my name illegibly, and tore the page out. He accepted it gracefully and did not offer me any pesos.

On the highway back to camp I wondered what would become of this boy who had entered our lives so easily. He had altered my perception of the brown children walking narrow dirt streets between tiny stucco buildings. I remembered the shame I had felt after forcing the pesos into his hands, and my anger that coins had entered a transaction in hummingbirds. But I was angrier still at my own society, in which money was the measure of success in every transaction, even those, maybe especially those, involving art and nature. He made a hummingbird because he was a person who molded his impressions of his environment, and the bird was at that moment an important part of the place he lived. I dreamed of returning to Mexico and finding an artist of power and assurance, a new generation's Diego Rivera, laying out in heroic murals the symbolism of his hopes and aspirations. In all his work you can see bougainvillea, and hummingbirds; they are personal reminders of his power to direct the behavior of those older, and presumably wiser, than he, just by making pictures.

14

Scammon's Lagoon

The mirage acts alive; always present, ever changing, it rests on the horizon, intruding between the sand and the sea like a fluid layer of mercurical quartz, flickering beneath the far-off boats, their drivers standing, pointing, their passengers huddled in the bow. The sun warms a low finger of dunes; heat waves shimmer in the distance, frustrating my efforts to focus binoculars. On the flats, marbled godwits stab again and again into the gray muck, stepping erratically but inexorably, and seemingly obliviously, toward where I sit, elbow braced on knees, trying to hold the glasses steady in the morning chill, staring into the eyepieces, imagining them to be on a brass telescope, and myself to be the first whaler to discover this place. The boats out on the lagoon suddenly change course and speed up. Behind me Rafe says, "There's a spout." A puff of mist appears above the mirage. I've just seen my first whale. My mind suddenly takes me back to the southern Oklahoma woods, where a former teacher, George M. Sutton, the famous ornithologist, stops, cocks his head, and says, "Hear that?" With a series of faint notes, every bit as far away and as ephemeral as the spout, I "see" my first warbler of the morning.

A Mercedes bus is parked a hundred yards away on the soft sand road. Earlier, in the RV park near the boundary between Baja California Norte and Baja California Sur, I watched this same bus perform its miracles. The sides folded down into a kitchen and a picnic table. Through the expansive windshield I could see the people inside; a stocky, topless woman was looking for, finding, and struggling into her bra. Then she found her jacket and came outside for breakfast. A raw wind blew in from the west; I sipped burning coffee and wiped cold tears out of my eyes. A little blond dog with open sores poked around my feet for scraps. My wet towel clung to the chain link fence where I had tied it the night before to dry. My head throbbed; throughout the night, one after another, Mexican semi drivers had roared along a nearby stretch of Highway 1, the *bla-a-a-a-p* of their unmuffled diesels making me dream of tired brown men pushing gears in a darkness cut only by their headlights and glowing cigarettes.

A young man, the German driver of the Mercedes bus, walked into our camp. He was leading a commercial bird-watching tour through Baja California.

"This is my first trip to America," he said, "but I memorized the pictures in the books and went to the museums, so I know the birds real well."

After a few minutes of conversation, it became obvious that this rookie was indeed qualified to lead a tour. He talked about the species he expected to see, the places he was taking the group, and the reasons why it was important for these German citizens to add species to their life lists. This all happened two hours ago. Now, at Scammon's Lagoon, we sit with binocs while the occupants of the Mercedes bus are out on the water in long wooden boats.

A flock of sandpipers flies low over the glassy water, long

wings whipping quickly through the layered, warming light, dark forms silhouetted against the hazy horizon. They come out of an endless alluvium — Laguna Ojo de Liebre, the Eye of the Rabbit — where the continent merges almost imperceptibly with the ocean to the south. Still flying, the birds disappear into the dune shadows to the north. Once more I realize how lucky I am to have seen shorebirds in my lifetime: avocets asleep, standing on a leg in the shallow brine, their repeated, reflected markings making an abstract copy of themselves; dunlins twisting and turning over a salt pond, their flashing underwings an explosion against an already bright sky; one black-bellied plover, his singularity accented by the dozens of other species around him. These scenes validate my decision to come to Mexico. A long, expensive flight, days of driving, night adjusting my old body to the unyielding ground, all are balanced by a flock of sandpipers, a spout against the distant dunes, and *barqueros* pointing in the mirage. At last I am sitting on the shore of Scammon's Lagoon. Rafe begins talking about whales.

Rafe Payne has chosen to give this lecture standing in front of the dunes at the end of a long and brutal road, beside the mirror water. He has brought his class to the very place where a whaler captain discovered the breeding grounds of gray whales, then used the unique lay of the land and the lagoon to ensure maximum slaughter. At other places in Baja California, Rafe's students have been introduced to geology, botany, malacology, the missionary experience, and Hispanic culture. Here at Scammon's Lagoon, they will learn something of the history, the sense of adventure, the isolation, danger, and audacity of whaling — an activity that symbolizes the darker side of our relationship with earth, namely the slaughter of physically enormous, highly intelligent mammals.

*

The killing of whales in the last century is a well-documented activity that probably comes as close as any in recorded history to the Stone Age butchering of mammoths. The size of a large elephant overlaps that of a small whale; each type of hunt was necessarily cooperative, involving the limits of technology; the tendons, ligaments, and bones of the prey are about the same strength and weight; and the animals are about equally able to wreak havoc on their tormentors. In the 1850s, Charles Scammon was among the most observant of those who chased great big animals with primitive weapons, and in his writings we have a businesslike description of the business. What Scammon saw in the lagoon and recorded for us was violence that regularly deteriorated into a surreal visual experience:

> Here . . . the scene of slaughter was exceedingly picturesque and unusually exciting, especially on a calm morning, when the mirage would transform not only the boats and their crews into fantastic imagery, but the whales, as they sent forth their towering spouts of aqueous vapor, frequently tinted with blood, would appear greatly distorted. At one time . . . both boats and whales would assume ever-changing forms, while the report of the bomb-guns would sound like the sudden discharge of musketry; but one can not fully realize, unless he be an eyewitness, the intense and boistrous excitement of the reckless pursuit.

The excitement did not come cheaply, nor without careful planning and provision. A well-equipped whaling voyage to the Baja California coast required one hundred and fifty bomb lances, an equal number of toggle harpoons, four bomb guns, thirty-five cast-steel lances. Once their prey was killed, the crew needed four grapnel hooks, three fluke chains, one fin chain, three head straps, and a "fish hook" to handle their catch. In anticipation of a successful hunt, "3500 barrels of oil casks" were stowed below deck. Whaling was a messy business: The ship carried eighteen hundred pounds of soap. Today we'd question Scammon's concern for his crew's health: He loaded on a thousand pounds of tobacco and a ton of butter. His medicine chest contained gallons of rum and brandy. To get his men going in the morning, he took twelve hundred pounds of coffee. He also specified some books for the ship's library. I find myself wondering about the titles of these books, and about who read them. But killing whales was evidently not all fun and games; Scammon recommended twelve pairs of handcuffs.

I suspect, however, that Cro-Magnon men hunting mammoths also shared some of Charles Scammon's practical knowledge. First, one needed to hit the right animal. The literary ship captain tells us:

> Another danger is, that in darting the lance at the mother, the young one, in its gambols, will get in the way of the weapon, and receive the wound, instead of the intended victim. In such instances, the parent animal, in her frenzy, will chase the boats, and, overtaking them, will overturn them with her head, or dash them in pieces with a stroke of her ponderous flukes.

The bomb gun, however, was a great improvement over the flint blades used twenty thousand years ago:

> The bomb-gun is made of iron, stock and all. It is three feet long, the barrel of which is twenty-three inches in length; diameter of bore, one and one eighth inch; weight, twenty-four pounds. It shoots a bomb-lance twenty-one and a half inches long . . . pointed at the ends, with sharpened edges, in order to cut its way through the fibrous fat and flesh . . . the gun is fired from the shoulder, in the same way as a musket.

A certain amount of luck was always welcome:

> As soon as the boat is fast, the officer goes into the head, and watches a favorable opportunity to shoot a bomb-lance. Should

this enter a vital part and explode, it kills instantly, but it is not too often this good luck occurs; more frequently two or three bombs are shot, which paralyze the animal to some extent, when the boat is hauled near enough to use the hand-lance. After repeated thrusts, the whale becomes sluggish in its motions; then going "close to," the hand-lance is set into its "life," which completes the capture. The animal rolls over on its side, with fins extended, and dies without a struggle.

Scammon's Lagoon, being one of the calving sites for the California gray whale, offered some unique opportunities to observe the behavior of parent and offspring:

> At other times, when the cub is young and weak, the movements of the mother are sympathetically suited to the necessities of her dependent offspring. It is rare that the dam will forsake her young one, when molested.

And what happens to the calves?

> Two, three, or more cubs have been seen with the California Grey Whale; but this has only happened in the lagoons where there had been great slaughter among the cows . . . A whale which had a calf perhaps a month old was killed close to the ship. When the mother was taken to the ship to be cut in, the young one followed, and remained playing about for two weeks.

Being in this place of such historical and biological importance, listening to Rafe give his lecture, I can visualize the distant action described so matter-of-factly by Charles Scammon. The *barqueros* seem transformed into whalers, the *touristas'* cameras become bomb-guns, the spouts turn red, and the ghost of Scammon's schooner, *Marin,* her sails mostly furled, lies waiting, split by the mirage, against the lagoon barrier.

This habit of letting my imagination take me into the past was formed at an early age. My grandfather's house contained a remarkable set of books on natural history. I remember lying on his living room floor as a child and staring at the pictures — insects metamorphosing, butterflies, fish, and so on. I studied one color plate time and time again, noting the details, the brush strokes, and the artistic technique of the illustrator. The scene was of a woolly mammoth being attacked by a band of skin-clad hunters armed with spears. The mammoth was throwing one of the men into the air with its trunk, smashing another with its feet. This painting became my private vision of prehistory. Fifteen thousand years after that event was supposed to have taken place, I sat on the shore of Ojo de Liebre Lagoon, realizing that Scammon's crews lived an experience similar to the one in the book:

> The murderous blow often causes the animal to recoil in its anguish, and give a swoop of its ponderous flukes, or a toss of its head, which, coming in contact with the boat, produces a general wreck . . . And out of eighteen men who officered and manned them, six were badly jarred, one had both legs broken, another three ribs fractured, and still another was so much injured internally that he was unable to perform duty during the rest of the voyage . . . all before a single whale was captured.

The nineteenth-century commercial whalers' technology is in stark contrast to that used about the same time by American Indians along the northern coasts. Picture a Nootkan whaler, heavy fur cape hanging to his ankles, cradling a harpoon as thick as a rural fence post and twice as long as he is tall. Slung over his back is a pair of sealskin floats attached to a sinew and cedar-bark rope nearly a hundred yards long. His weapon is tipped with a mussel shell blade. He is barefoot. With a little luck his companions will row to almost within arm's length of a gray whale. Then the man will strike.

The turn-of-the-century anthropologist and photographer Edward Curtis captured just such an individual on film; we don't know his name, but we do know that he, and those like him, did much more hunting than killing. A Nootkan chief called Maquinna went to sea for fifty-three days before bringing home a whale. He lost the first eight he hit and probably worried whether the ninth would sink before he landed it. Once an animal was harpooned, the hunters followed the floats until the whale died. Then one of the band jumped into the icy waters, cut a hole in the jaw, another in the upper lip, and tied the mouth closed. A dead gray whale with its mouth tied shut was less likely to sink than an open-mouthed one.

Scammon's writings and Curtis's photography give us a picture of grand adventure that seems more brutal, cold, dangerous, and at times outright foolhardy than thrilling. But even the Nootka found a way to hide the reality of hunting in myth. In one legend Tsahwasip the harpooner killed so many whales that they lay unused on the beach. There was so much meat that the people named him Yáhlua (the name of an ancestral chief), and his last wife bore a supernatural child who lived a life filled with travel, adventure, spirits, and magical experiences.

The iconography of success pervades our vision of the interactions between men and large mammals. The encyclopedia plate of mammoth hunters may well be one more example of the imagery of our relationships with nature fueling exploitation through use of the "conquer" concept. In this regard the painting is very similar to the entire record of whaling. Both the mammoth picture and the whaling literature suggest cooperation, male bonding, and the surmounting of an enormous challenge, all embedded in an acceptable social context. To the artist, mammoths were terrifying monsters, capable of hellish destruction. The men attacking them were doing so out of necessity — food, clothing, and provisions for their women and babies. We perceive these Pleistocene warriors as brave and undaunted, out on a vital mission. And whaling was a great business, too, while it lasted.

To conquer is to be noble and admired; to conquer against all odds is to be legendary. But to chase and strike and get bashed into ripped and shattered bloody bones, then chase and strike again and again without a kill, while squirrels and rabbits are abundant and the women wait, chewing nuts and berries, is perhaps more real. Yes, I think, how easy it is to paint a picture, either with pigments or words, that others will accept as true because they have never been to the places where the events occurred, never participated in the action, and want to believe what others tell them.

The actual killing and butchering of a very large animal brings humans into contact with a great deal of blood, freshly sliced skin, hot internal organs that continue to pulsate long after the violence has ended, and the deep, overpowering smell of intestinal contents. Today most of this kind of activity takes place in packing plants. Modern civilization has separated us intellectually from the world of wild creatures, except in one case: the destruction of large animals for political purposes, that is, war. Compared to whales and mammoths, we are small, but in truth we are relative giants; the typical occupant of earth is an insect. And throughout popular culture the image of successful attack against symbolic mammoths, the sallying forth to confront the modern whale-equivalents and thus preserve our way of life, is considered "action adventure." Our "entertainment" is laced through and through with the iconography of goodness against monstrosity.

But the romantic and mythical image of "adventure" has only recently been rendered vulnerable to evaluation by the cold, neutral, almost "scientific" eye of technology, that is, the twentieth-century camera. For example, Paul Fussell, in an article in *The Atlantic* (August 1989), tells us that in the picture book *Life Goes to War,* a "volume so popular and widely distributed as to constitute virtually a definitive and official anthology of Second World War photographs," there are no pictures of dismembered American soldiers. Fussell continues with a listing of "histories" in which "no matter how severely wounded, . . . everyone has all his limbs . . . not to mention an expression of courage and cheer." But the great adventure is really one of terror, friends blown to bits, and an insanity so extreme as to redefine the limits of the human mental experience. By the late 1950s John Steinbeck, who on the eve of the Holocaust had gone collecting in the Gulf of California, could write, in *Once There Was a War,* "I don't mean that correspondents are liars . . . It is in the things not mentioned that the untruth lies." There are no deluded colonels in the official version of hostilities. Steinbeck notes, "The foolish reporter who broke the rules would not be printed at home and in addition would be put out of the theater by the command."

Between 1950 and 1970 two important events occurred: The Korean War ended and the information explosion began. Korea taught me that neither generals nor Americans were invincible and that negotiations did not always proceed quickly and easily. I was not in Korea; I didn't learn such things firsthand. These principles were taught by simple pictures and one- or two-syllable words. Our family lived on the edge of Oklahoma City; once or twice a week a buddy and I walked a couple of miles to go hunting rabbits. We would stop at a one-pump rural filling station to buy candy bars. On the wall of that single-room wooden building was posted the daily newspaper map of Korea, with the Allied perimeter shrinking toward Pusan. Then the Marines invaded at Inchon. In seemingly quick succession, the Allies swept northward and the oceans of Chinese chased them back south. MacArthur was relieved of duty by President Truman. My mother and I sat in the living room and listened to the old-soldier speech. I didn't need a textbook to tell me what we as a nation were about in Korea. Douglas MacArthur, advocating all-out war with the most populous nation on earth, came home to a "hysterical welcome from a country that still loved him." The pictures and words spread with stunning speed and effect into the far reaches of the Sooner State. Even Oklahoma high school boys had an opinion on Truman's act, and most of us felt MacArthur was in the right. In MacArthur's own words: "My welcome throughout the entire land defies description." But many years later Neil Sheehan wrote that the general had "wrapped himself too artfully in the flag . . . and his excuses were too eloquent for Americans to see his flaws." Douglas MacArthur had dragged home the vanquished mammoth; his casks were filled with sperm oil.

Our family acquired its first television set in 1952. I was well prepared for this event, having watched a great deal of test pattern at the houses of more affluent friends in my preadolescent years. By 1970 nearly every American household had at least one television set, and you had to get up at odd hours to find a test pattern. If certain images of men engaged in far-off noble adventure became suspect in Korea, they were destroyed in Vietnam. Generals' claims, made in front of live television cameras, were easily evaluated by an electorate with ready access to the brutally democratic eye of new information-processing technology. The repertoire of Vietcong booby traps, trip wires, pungi sticks, and other products of an ingenious agrarian people at war in their sub-tropical homeland with a culturally naive invader, quickly became known to the general public half a world away. Eventually the word "Vietnam" would become a metaphor in the American political vocabulary.

*

Back at Ojo de Liebre, listening to Rafe's words, remembering Scammon's prose, blunt as an uncut satellite transmission,
I conclude that humanity is on the verge of metamorphosis.
We have changed from a species that derives its motivation
from direct interaction with the real world of nature, into one
that makes decisions, then acts, on the basis of easily manipulated electronic images. Our collective inability to hide the
"truth," as in the example of the Chinese slaughter of their
own peacefully demonstrating citizens in Tiananmen Square,
is matched by our unprecedented power to create fantasy,
from movie special effects to docudramas. A large fraction of
us consider pure entertainment worthy of fairly serious attention. Out of the thirty most-watched television programs in
history (up to the start of the Iraq war), thirteen were football
games. Two were Bob Hope Christmas specials, and another
was a segment of the evening soap opera "Dallas." Through
the end of the 1980s the two most popular syndicated shows
in the United States, as the nation silently watched the disintegration of political systems throughout Eastern Europe,
were game shows: "Wheel of Fortune" and "Jeopardy!"

The heaviest electronic narcotic users are women fifty-five
years and older, who spend an average of twenty-seven hours
a week in front of the tube. Men in powerful decision-making
positions — televangalists and presidents, secretaries of the
treasury and state, governors, U. S. senators, chairmen of the
boards of Chrysler, Ford, and General Motors, heads of major defense contractor corporations, presidents of agribusi-
ness conglomerates — tend to be in that same age group.
While the wives are home watching "Jeopardy!" — statisti-
cally speaking, of course — the husbands are out in the physical world inventing the leveraged buyout and wreaking havoc
with savings and loan companies, aquifers, forests, and the
ozone layer. If my trip to Scammon's Lagoon has accomplished anything, it is to remind me once more of the incred-

ible mystic beauty that can surround massive destruction, first carried out in the name of business and politics, then painted with the glow of masculine adventure.

Down the shore, taking notes and listening intently, sits the next generation. I wonder what effect this visit to Charles Scammon's killing fields will have on these students, and whether that effect will stay with them when they take their places among the nation's leaders and decision makers. Rafe Payne spreads a map on the sand; he talks about whale migrations, feeding habits, reproductive behavior. On their breeding grounds, gray whales may seem friendly, investigating skiffs and letting tourists pet their snouts, but a more objective appraisal of their behavior suggests they are attracted by the sound of an idling outboard. They tend to leave when the engine is shut off. They also sometimes get pushy, shoving the boats in an increasingly forceful manner. We have no way whatsoever of understanding these acts; the whales' size, and the circumstances under which they live, preclude the kind of experimental research that helps us explain strange behavior in other species. But in general it is a mistake to interpret animal behavior in human terms. As smart and curious as they are, gray whales do not have our practices, morals, values. They are wild animals faced with the problems of being very large and living in the ocean.

We all sit in silence and listen. The morning is dead calm. From far across the glassy surface comes a sound, a deep and mighty sigh — the sound of a gray whale breathing, a sound of great exhalation that is thirty million years old. How far the earth has come, I think, from the Cambrian seas, how much has changed, how many forms have lived for millions of years, then disappeared forever. And how little most of us understand where we truly fit in that parade of success and failure.

15

Mechanics

R afe's teaching assistant, Rick Murrane, is a man of many talents: scuba diver, van wrangler, boat jockey. Rick's mechanical troubles started a little way south of Los Angeles, but he didn't think they were serious, so he kept driving. When the three-vehicle caravan stopped to gas up, change money, and buy insurance at San Ysidro, the problem hadn't gotten much worse; Rick and Rafe talked things over for quite a while before deciding to go on. Then the border worked its magic.

"It's missing pretty bad and I'm losing power." Rick's voice over the CB radio had a certain matter-of-factness about it. This is not a real problem, said the inflection, something minor, maybe dirt in the carburetor; it'll work its way through. A few minutes later he was back on the horn.

"I don't think we can make it up this hill."

"We'll pull off and wait," said Rafe into the microphone. He selected a turnout high above the Pacific Ocean. The road cut revealed a wonderful set of formations — the past effects of geological processes at work and their mimics produced by bulldozers: Tertiary conglomerates and ancient beaches next to mixed gravel roadbed fill. An elegant velvet cactus sprawled on the ridge behind the van; I selected a short telephoto lens to compose the pattern of stems against a bright sky with interesting cloud. Far below, beyond a complex winding and falling arroyo littered with cans, wrappers, and toilet paper, gentle Pacific waves washed against a narrow beach. At the horizon yellow-white haze rested on a calm sea. I traded camera for binoculars and searched for whales. Gulls passed through the field of view.

Some of the students started walking down the canyon toward the beach. I dropped the binoculars to watch their progress, wondering whether I had time to join them before Rick arrived and, with my expert help, fixed the minor problem, using our ingenuity and insight into the operations of our most familiar machines. Always curious about the interactions between humans and their environment, I studied the trash scattered below me. Two-thirds of the way to the bottom of this rugged gully lay what looked to be the skeleton of a Datsun. The yellow steel box was like a specter from my past. Our daughter had purchased a nearly identical industrial artifact in California, then had wired it together for a migration across the mountains to the prairies. A year later she bought a west-bound train ticket back to Oakland.

"Sell it if you can," she said on the platform at three in the morning, adding no further advice or instructions. Back home, in the daylight, I pried open the hood with a screwdriver and studied the engine. Then I placed an ad in the newspaper. A mother and teenager showed up; the child looked as if she had passed her driver's test that day. I watched them struggle into the torn front seats; the little car lurched down the street and out of sight. Suddenly the neighborhood seemed clean and silent.

Half an hour later they were back. I wrote out a bill of sale. The mother smiled, serene and happy; the young girl seemed almost aroused. Love is truly blind. She counted out four hundred dollars' worth of twenties. I imagined the money accumulating slowly and painfully in a dresser drawer, from baby sitting and other minimum-wage jobs, over a several-year period measured in resisted clothes purchases and deferred fast food orgies. I signed the odometer statement, then gave her the bill of sale, title, and a second set of keys.

"I can get it notarized," said the mother.

I watched from the bedroom window as the daughter soloed toward the main arterial into town. All the words we had ever said to our own children as they made their rites of passage — alone in the most pervasive, seductive, and deadly piece of technology a civilized nation has ever placed in the hands of its citizens — came back to me as the yellow Datsun disappeared, forever, I thought at the time, around a curve.

Standing beside the four-lane north of Ensenada, looking down at the wreck, all the guilt I had felt that day came back to mind. The Datsun had apparently returned in an attempt to haunt me. But instead of the evil spirit settling on my shoulders, Rick and, by association, Rafe, were paying for my sins. I had never forgotten the face of that girl, her expression at having bought a car of her own. I'd been sobered, a little frightened, by the sight of a person walking, eyes wide open, into an intimate, costly, and all-consuming relationship with a machine. I was reminded of the opening paragraphs in Freeman Dyson's book *Disturbing the Universe,* in which he relates the story of a child, Philip, whose wooden block city comes alive at night. In this magic city the boy can wish for anything, but if he asks for technology, he has to keep it forever. With remarkable wisdom, Philip chooses a horse instead of a bicycle.

I focused my binoculars on the car body below. Two or three of the students gathered around it; one stuck his head into the glassless window. Then they went on down to the beach. It goes without saying that in Baja California abandoned vehicles are stripped. But there is a human cost to mechanical failure. Experienced Baja travelers can entertain any crowd of rookies with the following legend: A man retired, bought an RV, converted his life savings into cash, and headed for some serene, secluded, and picturesque haven to finish out his days on earth. Somewhere in the middle of the peninsula his mobile retirement home caught fire, and he lost everything but his life. I asked Rafe what the man did then. Rafe shrugged. I got the sense that figuring out what people do *after* vehicle disasters in Mexico is part of a mental game.

The third van came limping up the long hill. Rafe opened the trailer and got out his tool box. From Rick's description of his problems, I had diagnosed the cause: worn choke linkage, which allowed the plate to flop closed and flood the hot engine. Solution: wire the thing open, preferably with a bent coat hanger. Then the trip could proceed for the next three weeks with no more hitches. This kind of fantasy is a product of my marriage. My father-in-law had an artistic touch with automobiles. In retrospect, I realize that we saw only this side of him, saw the problems that yielded quickly to his enormous insight and experience and thus got fixed with a screwdriver. If you ask his surviving relatives what they remember most about him, they'll tell you of his knack for performing mechanical miracles.

"My car is real hard to start, Glenn," I said to him one time. He pulled out the distributor wire, cut a half inch off with his pocket knife, stuck a straight pin into the end of the wire, then put it back into the distributor. He reached through the window and flicked the ignition. The old Ford started on the first crank.

"What do I owe you for this three minutes' worth of work?" He grinned and bit on his pipe. I got the feeling that he wanted me to understand how easy it is, when dealing with deadly and expensive toys, for minor problems to turn into major ones. Or he wanted to warn me that if I was determined to play with these toys at seventy miles an hour without that understanding, then to get ready for some trouble.

These were the kinds of memories that flashed through my mind as Rafe opened the tool box and started digging, and Rick unclipped the engine cowl inside the van. One by one, all the males in the group took their looks, rendered their opinions, and backed off, waiting for the next miracle worker. Finally I asked for a piece of wire.

"Starts to miss and cut out as the engine heats up," I said, reminding the befuddled group of the symptoms. "Chances are it's a worn automatic choke linkage." Sure enough, the linkage was worn; I rattled it to demonstrate, then wired the plate open. Like a true believer, Rick replaced the cowl.

"Let's load up." Rafe looked at his watch. The people who had gone down to the beach came back up over the edge of the little canyon.

"Nice Datsun?" I joked about the trash below.

"It was a Toyota," said one of the students. "On top of a new Porsche and a family sedan of some kind. Looks like they got stuck right here" — he surveyed our vans, trailer, and boat — "then got stripped and rolled off. This fixed?"

"Worn choke linkage. Wired it open."

We pulled out into traffic. The van seemed to run satisfactorily. My father-in-law would have been proud of me, I thought. Of course, in the hour we had taken to work on it, the engine had cooled.

By the time we reached Ensenada, the CB conversation revealed that no miracle had been performed. We waited in a shopping-center parking lot while Rafe and Rick went in search of a mechanic. Two hours later, having exhausted the local *panadería*'s supply of fresh tortillas, we left Rick in the company of a man named Antonio and drove south to camp at Estero Beach. Sometime in the early morning hours, Rick's headlights appeared on the road into camp. He stepped down triumphantly.

"All fixed! The man's a genius!"

Antonio's house had an overhanging roof in front, beneath which was the shop. There were no manuals, no diagnostic electronics, no visible supply of spare parts. A van identical to Rick's sat next to the shed. Antonio drove Rick's van up onto a ramp to get under it. He checked the fuel pump by sucking and blowing on the gas lines. He checked for shorts by putting his hands on various wires to see if he got a shock. They waited until dark so Antonio could see the firing off the tips of plug wires, thus finding out whether electricity was getting to the cylinders. In the darkness he discovered sparks arcing between plug wires and recommended that Rick get some new ones. Then they went for a drive with the inside cowl off, the chunky asphalt and thrown gravel roaring up through the opening at their feet, yelling at one another over the noise. Antonio put his hand on the coil, decided it was too hot, and cooled it with a wet rag. At two in the morning, Rick was in total awe of a Mexican stranger he'd met the evening before.

"Needed a new coil. That's all it was, bad coil. Took him a while to find the part."

Later, reflecting back on Ensenada, Rick would give Antonio his due: "He said that if it wasn't fixed, to bring it back and he'd work on it free. Well, maybe he didn't fix it, but he didn't make it any worse."

South of San Vincente, Rafe admitted defeat.

"Take it back to Los Angeles," he told Rick as we put three vans' worth of gear and humans into two. "We'll look for you in Bahía in a couple of days." He put his arm around Rick's shoulder and said a prayer. Then we went south and Rick went north. Shortly after we parted, a fan blade broke off in Rick's engine, crashing through the engine compartment and clipping a transmission-fluid cooling line, whereupon the red fluid spewed out on the highway. Rick pulled off on a curve with no apron, right wheels in the ditch, left ones on the blacktop, and stepped across the road to flag a ride.

Thirty minutes later a black car with Mexican plates roared past us, an American arm waving frantically from the passenger's side. We turned off the highway. Rick hopped out and thanked the grinning driver. Rafe unhooked his trailer and drove back north with Rick, leaving us by the side of the road with one vehicle, a boat, a trailer, and three vans of people. It seemed to me that we were losing at this game; our options were disappearing at a fairly rapid rate. Strange birds flitted through the nearby brush. Across some dry fields stood a hacinda; its occupants were nowhere to be seen. A hundred yards from where we'd stopped was a burned-out bus. Directly across the highway a perfect buckhorn cholla posed in classic grace. I looked up at the sky. In three more hours the light would be perfect. I saw the picture in my mind: cactus against the dark hill, with spines backlighted in the setting sun.

A few miles to the north, Rafe left Rick at the disabled van and drove to town for transmission fluid, convinced that a quart would get them into San Vicente. It did, but in the five miles of driving with an unbalanced fan, the water pump went out. Antifreeze gushed out steaming onto the reddish clay in front of the police station. Rafe paid the cops twenty dollars to watch the van. They agreed to watch it for one night. Then Rafe drove to Ensenada, where they located a flatbed truck whose owner, Manuel, told Rick his life story: Manuel's friends still called him *cuate* — twin, or buddy — although his brother had died when they were fifteen. At the San Vicente police station, Manuel loaded the van onto the truck and started back to Ensenada. He and Rick agreed that the proper thing to do was to at least stop by Antonio's. The flatbed pulled up beside the overhang; Antonio came out; Rick and Manuel walked around to the back of the truck. The three men then stared up at the van with the dumbfounded dismay that accompanies encounters with the supernatural. The van's engine was running.

"This van has a ghost in it," ventured Antonio. He invited Rick to eat dinner and spend the night. The next morning Manuel hauled the haunted machine to the border.

Meanwhile we proceeded south to San Quintín, then on to Bahía de los Ángeles. The Ocañas' auto paint and repair business, casting colored reflections in the bright morning light next to the Vermilion Sea Field Station, symbolized the Baja Californian interaction with automobiles, a relationship that contrasted sharply with that of the typical American. Meginnis Ford, a few blocks from my own home in Nebraska, is a sanitized agency that hides its garage work behind a layer of smooth-talking service managers and doesn't take checks. At seven-thirty in the morning, most of the customers in the Meginnis shop are likely to be well-dressed people without the time, tools, expertise, or inclination to fix their own automobiles. They have spent upwards of fifteen thousand dollars for a steel box on wheels, and they want it to start in the winter and get them to work. The Ocañas' yard seemed to be more in tune with Antonio's approach to vehicular problems than with that I'd expect to find back home. Surely, I thought, studying the parts and gutted bodies, I'm seeing either bravado or magic. If anything drove out of that yard in the next few days. I would give my neighbors credit for the latter.

In the yard, like a gigantic abstract assemblage, lay a stack of car and truck doors, various headlight frames, brake drums and shoes, gas tanks, seats (upside down), a couple of engine blocks, mufflers and tailpipes, valve covers, springs, front suspensions, pickup tailgates, a stack of hoods (mostly Ford), oil pans, heavy extension cords running through it all, an air-pressure hose coming out of the house, cylinder heads, plastic oil containers, wiper blades, distributors with multi-colored plug wires still attached, differentials, ring gears, and rear axles. In one area was a crazy pile of small engines — from generators and pumps, I guessed; there were no power lawn mowers in Bahía de los Ángeles. This material was moved about, sorted, and inventoried as necessary, by means of hands, a block-and-pully rope winch, and a broken saw-horse.

The preferred work surface is a plywood square on top of a fifty-five-gallon drum, although the engines, when pulled, are laid at a crazy angle on a sturdy four-foot-square table. Today, if he gets the part from Guerrero Negro, Roberto Ocaña will replace the head gasket on a Datsun. Tomorrow he will do a brake job on a big truck. A Ford Courier pickup is getting new paint. Ruben is the body specialist; he routinely transforms old ones into new. I have a rare opportunity to study this work at close range; for some unexplained reason, the VSFS outhouse is in the middle of the Ocañas' business.

A 1963 Falcon sits next to the latrine; behind it is a 1967 Plymouth. The VW beetle beside them belongs to a visitor. North of the beetle is a 1964 Comet, a 1964 Chevy two-door, and a 1972 Mercury Monterey. Beside the main work shed is a 1952 Ford station wagon. West of the wagon is the front half of an adobe building, a forties pickup with a wooden stake bed, a World War II military three-quarter-ton pickup, and an amphibious landing craft. In addition to the Datsun, a metallic blue early-seventies Dodge Coronet sits in the main part of the work yard, tires flat, hood up, engine lying nearby on a sheet of plywood.

The Ocañas are doing an overhaul on the Dodge — rings and so on — working without electricity until the town generator comes on about ten or ten-thirty. Sunday mornings are the best times for these mechanics. They all seem happier than they are during the week; the atmosphere is almost festive. There in the bright sunshine, radios blaring trumpets backed by the deep resonance of big guitars, beer bottles set among the hoses and steel, Roberto, Ruben, and whatever friends happen to drop by get their hands dirty. What I see from the VSFS window resembles nothing so much as a group of my fellow scientists messing around with their equipment, trying to solve a problem, produce a tangible accomplishment they can point to with pride. In the end my friends' successes appear in learned journals; the Ocañas' drive away.

"¡*Buenos dias, Roberto!*"

"*Juanito.*" He lifts his chin slightly, squints. I inquire about the Datsun. He shakes his head; the gasket still hasn't come from Guerrero Negro and isn't likely to arrive on a Sunday morning. Where did he learn his mechanics? From his father, he answers, the Arnulfo Ocaña who kept the mine engines running and the ore cars moving down the narrow tracks.

"Ever work on fuel-injected engines?" I ask him.

His expression turns puzzled, quizzical. I don't know whether the problem is language, the technology we're discussing, or perhaps the subtle cultural interaction among people, language, and machines.

"Diesel?" he answers. I remember that I have not seen many Mexicans driving cars with fuel-injected gasoline engines.

"Front-wheel-drive cars?" I ask. "Transaxles?"

A blank look comes over his face. When he responds, I'm not sure whether he has rendered a personal opinion or passed judgment on America's enslavement by the scientific ignorance that permeates my culture:

"New cars are no good. Old cars are best. Fords and Chevys." He glances over at the Datsun and shakes his head again.

While "old Fords and Chevys" may be the favored chariots in Roberto's mind, in the late 1980s the most popular American conveyances were the Ford Escort, upon which humans made a capital investment of about three billion dollars, and the Ford Taurus, for another four billion. I don't know what it costs to get your car fixed at the Ocañas', but across the border to the north drivers spend at least forty billion dollars a year on maintenance and service. My Ford mechanic father-in-law always said the shop profits covered the losses in the sales department. Which is why we always took our machines to him: In a place like El Reno, Oklahoma, you had to do quality work to survive. I suspect the same holds true for Bahía de los Ángeles. But such trustworthiness is not always easy to find. There are at least two hundred offices and agencies where you can file a complaint if you think you have been defrauded on repairs. But most of us solve our serious transportation problems by getting new, or at least different, cars. Which is what Rick did, too. In a couple of days he showed up at the Vermilion Sea Field Station in another van.

Automobiles serve as transportation, income tax write-offs, impromptu bedrooms, hobbies, status symbols, grounds for divorce, nostalgia trips, movie props, excuses, and slave mothers. In their latter role they do common tasks for us that we could easily do ourselves, such as telling us when our key is in the ignition and the door is open, calculating our gas mileage and our trip mileage, reminding us to buckle our seat belts, even strapping the belt across our chest when we turn on the ignition, sounding an alarm when jostled by a presumptive thief, and inflating an air bag to save our lives when we hit something. Given all these luxuries, it didn't surprise me much that when Rick showed up with the new van, all the girls wanted to ride with him.

The rest of our technological enterprise has many of the same general properties as the automobile industry, a good example being the space shuttle program. The shuttles age and depreciate and are put out of commission by seemingly minor failures such as leaky O-rings. Although sold to voters as scientific equipment, the shuttles are inordinately expensive relative to their scientific value. Freeman Dyson, America's leading philosopher of technology, in his book *Infinite in All Directions,* shrugs off the shuttle program as more politics than science, claiming that if the nation really understood the goals of research, we would invest in less expensive unmanned multifunction explorers. He tags the same label on the Hubble Space Telescope — outdated, too restricted in its capacities, too much money for the scientific return.

Nor does Dyson confine his analysis to space vehicles. The upscaling of submarine-sized nuclear reactors into massive electrical generating stations brought design and safety problems, and with them a public fear that hamstrings us in our struggle with a rational energy policy. Is it stretching the point to suggest that an automobile capable of buckling a seat belt for you seduces you into believing you're being "taken care of"? I think not, but more realistically, an automatic seat belt is only one of thousands, maybe millions, of pervasive "conveniences" that minute by minute reinforce our intellectual separation from the task of staying alive, of successfully meeting the challenges we face. And when science fails — to cure cancer, develop an AIDS vaccine, clean up the environment, provide health, wealth, and longevity — it seems we turn to myths and morality plays, which are no more effective than machinery.

The fundamental problem, of course, is not with technology itself, but with our flawed vision of its powers and practice. Watching the activities outside the VSFS door, I must conclude that Roberto Ocaña could never be convinced that machinery was the only mark of highly civilized society. And some people think of Mexico as backward.

At four o'clock on a moonless January morning, lying on a cot wedged between specimen-laden shelves and a table piled with diving gear, my eyes open at the command of an internal alarm. A flashlight beam, fragmented by fingers held over the lens, darts through the pitch blackness, working its way into the room. Glen shakes my foot. It's time for some of us to start home; a day-long drive to the United States — with ritual dropping of money in Ensenada — lies ahead. We are leaving Rafe and his California students in Mexico and going back to San Diego, where Glen has made reservations on the whale-watch boat *Avanti*. Rafe may drive us to Scammon's Lagoon for a lecture and a spout, but Glen will guarantee us a back and a fluke, or your money's returned.

Outside, at the edge of the Ocañas' yard, a van stands waiting, sleeping bags and luggage piled to the windows, students crammed in between. Rafe pours us coffee and wishes us a safe trip. I look back for a last time at the car bodies, engines, and parts, more impressions than outlines in the gray-black predawn air. Tamarisk branches wave across my face, as they did when I first entered Bahía. In the next few hours I will cross deserts, mountains, and the line between a culture that performs daily surgery on the most hazardous discarded devices of its neighbor and another culture evolved to the point of virtually total dependency on people trained to try to repair those same devices.

Later in the day, along Mexico Highway 1 north of Cataviña, I walk across the blacktop to study one of the hundreds of small crosses that are distributed along that highway. This one is made of wrought iron; it is freshly painted, and plastic flowers were stuck into the upright column. I read the little sign. Roberto Navela was twenty-one years old when he failed to negotiate this blind hairpin curve.

Eventually I called Rafe to inquire about Rick's van.

"They completely rewired it, redid the whole electrical system." I assumed he was talking about factory-trained mechanics in Los Angeles.

"Was it fixed?"

"No. They overhauled the transmission, too."

"Was that the trouble?"

"No, the track team took it on a trip and had the same problems we did."

"Rafe, what, in fact, was wrong with that van?"

"This model has two fuel filters, one up front, which I think Antonio changed in Ensenada, and one way in the back, near the gas tank. When they changed the back one, it ran perfectly. Hasn't given anyone any more trouble. We'll probably take it back to Mexico next year."

16

Life Long Dreams

Beyond land's end, at the corner of Garrison and Scott streets in San Diego, lies a seascape built mostly of money, steel, and fiberglass. A forest of masts, outriggers, and antennas gives way in the distance to the fleet's mountains: military vessels, gray green in the morning sun, and behind their craggy profiles a pale haze. Nestled against her berth, responding gently to an imperceptible sighing of the bay, sits the *Avanti*. She is a magnificent piece of machinery with which to chase your lifelong dreams. Her woodwork is varnished and polished; her fiberglass is white and thick; no corrosive stains wash down her immaculate flanks. She has a bar, well stocked and clean — beer for dad, Diet Coke for mom, and Mountain Dew for the kids. Above the bar is a television set; if you choose, you can sit inside, have a drink, and watch a whale video instead of a whale. Or you can rent *Avanti* for a reception, invite your friends on board for a drink, and never leave the marina. And for only twelve dollars you can go to sea in search of *Eschrichtius robustus,* the California gray whale.

In addition to Glen Dappen and his students, my companions on this day include a group of men in their thirties, dressed in pleated cotton pants, semi-expensive jogging shoes, and rugby shirts covered by nondescript windbreakers; these men would melt easily into the crowd on an Omaha public golf course. One of them is wearing a Chicago Bears cap. He clearly envisions himself as the entertainment; a long string of off-color jokes issues from his mouth, followed by laughter from his buddies. I have long since stopped being surprised at the insecurity men feel in the company of people who want to see, and perhaps study, a wild plant or animal. Nor am I any longer shocked at the ribald humor that seems to accompany certain feelings of inadequacy. What is it about the words for sexual acts, bodily secretions and excretions, that relieve psychological discomfort? I don't know. This guy's mother should have told him: When you get on the *Avanti* to go watch whales, shut up; you will be surrounded by young women and children.

I find a place at the bow railing. Eight western grebes course through the glassy water below, diving, popping up, twisting their heads and necks, moving in and out through the spaces next to sailing yachts, sport fishing boats, and cruisers. Looking directly down on eight western grebes is as rare an experience as going to Lower California in the company of a master teacher. Our captain has yet to start his engines, and for me the trip is already worth its ticket price. An immature gull squawks repeatedly at an adult, begging, haranguing, demanding. This incident occurs in January, so the young gull is several months old, which makes me wonder how long gull parents have to put up with spoiled brat offspring who can't find a bird job.

Next to the *Avanti* the *Royal Polaris* sports a forest of fishing poles, clipped to the side of her main cabin like pool cues. Long gaff hooks are stacked against the front. The poles and reels for hire are ultramodern, top of the line for tourists seeking their brief taste of Hemingway. The gaffs are primitive tools; they look well used, out of the last century, if not unearthed from an Iron Age archeological site. Three narrow streams of water pour from six holes on the *Royal Polaris*'s stern; what internal mechanism selects the holes from which water pours on a sport fishing boat? Scientists ask these kinds of questions. The *Royal Polaris*'s radar bar rotates — military technology co-opted by the leisure-time industry. In the next berth *Champ* looks as if she has suffered an accident; the telltale signs of repaired fiberglass cover her bow. Across the traffic channel the *Yardarm* rocks slowly, her sail cover and boom swinging gently. The *Avanti*'s engines catch; I feel their vibrations in my feet and through my spine braced against the rail.

The Bears fan's sharp voice cuts through the others around me: a mixture of accents, Middle Eastern to Mississippian, with three kids from Edmonton chattering in clipped Canadian English. A young man in black leather jacket tries out the long lenses on his camera; a friend in fluorescent green mirror sunglasses helps him. Across the water a pelican stands on a light pole; old men with Styrofoam cups watch from the park bench on shore; Hispanics with boat names on their coveralls aim hoses over the dock boards or lean against the dock railing, smoking and waiting for their charters to leave. The grebes make their way, diving, surfacing, toward Harbor Island. Forster's terns slice the air, dropping to stab at fingerlings near the surface. The *Avanti* backs out of her berth, turns, and moves into the channel between Harbor Island and the naval base. An Arctic loon rides the wake, staring up at the faces peering over the rail. In the iridescent scum a dead merganser floats belly up, head and bill hanging down, opaque eyes staring into the darkness below. Talk among my shipmates turns to biology:

"Isn't it whales that have blubbers?" one woman asks her companion.

"I don't know," the other woman answers.

"Isn't that what they were taking them for, their blubbers?"

"I think so; that sounds right."

A military helicopter passes overhead. A hefty, well-dressed man draped with camera equipment takes picture after picture of this aircraft, aiming his telephoto lens like an admiring weapon; then he stands watching the sky, listening. This is the end of the twentieth century in America. If the helicopter is our visual symbol of military misadventure, its sound is our audible one. Close your eyes; even a kid with an electronic keyboard can take you back to Southeast Asia. The sound is overlaid on unflinching lyrics: Pink Floyd starts with electronic blades, which then lead to "we don't need no education." Overhead the whacking gets louder, then fades, repeatedly, as the rotary traffic over San Diego harbor picks up. The man with the telephoto lenses continues, silently, to focus, shoot, wind; his face serious and studious, he lights a cigarette.

Our tour guide greets us over the loudspeaker: "Welcome to the *Avanti* whale-watch boat. The *Avanti* operates under a policy of zero tolerance. If you are caught with drugs or paraphernalia, the authorities will meet us at the dock and take you away. Under California law, the boat owner can sue you for loss of income."

As we surge past the Harbor Island restaurant and toward Point Loma, a flock of sandpipers darts through the tangle of masts and shrouds. These birds remind me of a day when I was walking along a hot crystal beach beside the vast Lake McConaughy, a virtual inland paradise resting like a sterile mirror on the gray-green dunes of the Nebraska sandhills. My eye caught an unnatural movement a hundred yards ahead. I ran to find a western sandpiper wrapped up in a monofilament line stretched from a fishing pole whose owner was nowhere in sight. With thousands of miles of prairie across which to fly, this bird had the bad luck to hit a six-pound-test line at thirty miles an hour and get caught. I freed the animal from entanglement, looked into its dark eyes, let some nearby kids touch it, gave them the requisite unrequested biology lesson, and opened my hand. The sandpiper disappeared down the shore.

Then I thought about lifelong dreams, especially about how much of their fulfillment rested on effort or on chance. That bird had spent its whole life in wild toil, flying across continents, searching for food, finding, courting, and keeping a mate, feeding young, and flying great distances again. Then it hit a fishing line, *one* line, a few minutes before I walked down the beach. The difference between life and death was the congruency of unlikely random events. But maybe these happenings were not so unlikely after all. I walk shorelines all the time; western sandpipers fly them routinely; monofilament lines are an ever-present danger — I had seen many loons and grebes caught in them. And in summer children play on the sand. The chance that they would get to touch a sandpiper was, after all, calculable; it was about as likely as my being on the *Avanti* as a result of saying "I'd like to redo the Steinbeck trip."

The navy base lies low on our left, sealed off from the harbor by a chain link fence topped with barbed wire. Several large, ominous pipes issue from beneath the military installation and empty into the harbor. These drains are rusted, about four feet in diameter, and strengthened by circular ridges. Our guide reviews the history of submarine security; the navy no longer uses underwater nets for protection against enemy submarines, she tells us. The man with the telephoto

lenses continues to take pictures of helicopters and submarines, the latter at rest, almost like whales asleep, at their
tenders. The guy in the Bears cap switches from humor to
commentary on military equipment. Then I notice that all
around me people are taking pictures of helicopters and submarines. Everything from Instamatics to Polaroids to state-
of-the-art Nikons, in the hands of men, women, and children,
recording — for what posterity? — United States Navy ord-
nance.

A pair of jet fighters passes overhead; more photographs.
An older woman studies the war machines, her face solemn.
She stares for a long time at the helicopters; I wonder if she
knows someone whose fighter went down in the Tonkin Gulf
and who was then rescued at sea. For this woman's generation
"America" is almost synonymous with surviving the Great
Depression, victory in World War II, conquest of the Nazis
and the unbelievable horror they wrote into human history,
possession of an invincible nuclear arsenal, freedom, democracy, wealth, and Christianity. Studying her face, I sense that
the whipping concussion of helicopter blades does not put
this older woman at ease. Instead it suggests a level of technology, especially in the military, that she doesn't understand. But neither she nor I can escape the sounds of the
blades. They are as much a part of our audio culture as the
pumping base of small pickups filled with speakers, the relentless pulse of rap, the lonely smoothness of Spanish, the
shaved gentility of Chinese-English.

The crowd on the *Avanti* is as varied as the species; their
presence is a reflection of the changing colors of America,
the human movements that are called political but are probably more fundamentally biological. In a crowded world, where
cultures interact in many ways and the helicopter is a symbol
for flight in all directions, neither the flow of genes nor the

diffusion of ideas can be stopped. Yet we've all come together for an afternoon to watch whales; in three hours, no matter what our backgrounds, we'll have a common experience, something to talk about that all can agree upon. The tour guide calls our attention to Point Loma, a lighthouse put too far inland; ships, trusting its signals, ran aground. Sea lions are draped, snoozing, on red buoys.

Out on the open ocean we're encouraged to look for spouts and yell "thar she blows!" if we see one, reenacting — in Nike Air Jordans and Calvin Klein jeans — the adrenergic call of a burned and weatherbeaten Ishmael clinging to his stomach-wrenching perch. Of course our announcer spots the first one. Beneath my feet the engine hums higher, and the *Avanti* smoothly turns seaward and northward. All the talk from the Bears fan has stopped — the stories about when he was in the service, the submarines and Superbowl, his trip to Hong Kong, his car, his fishing expedition to Canada. The announcer tells us that it's a federal offense to chase whales too closely. I notice that *Invader, Mascot VI, Geisha,* and *Morning Star* have joined the *Avanti,* along with a scattering of Boston Whalers and other small boats, headed toward the horizon where someone saw a spout. I wonder if, hidden from my ears, this commercial fleet radios whale locations, or if they have a helicopter to tell them where to go, letting us believe we've really found one on our own.

The *Avanti*'s engines slow. Through the quiet, idling gurgle I hear another boat's announcer reciting facts originally gathered by Charles Scammon. We're told to aim our cameras at a slick patch on the water; the female voice softens — like the whisper of a television announcer at the crucial putt in a golf tournament. A dark back breaks the surface, slowly, easily, gliding through a gentle arc; from around the deck comes a collective gasp, then cheers, as the fluke hangs, and thirty shutters snap in unison. I've *seen* a whale, a real live wild whale, not just the spout; here before me is the actual creature, not just irrefutable evidence of its presence.

"You get some good pictures?" asks Glen as he reloads. His telephoto lens looks a yard long.

Pictures of lifelong dreams? A fluke above the water, dark backs, and a pair of V-shaped spouts against the yellow haze?

"I think so."

He offers to give me copies of his photographs, should mine not turn out. Glen makes his world go around by giving: his time, care, consideration, ideas, observations, field notes, slides, videotapes, Spanish-lesson cassette tapes, experience with hauling other people's children into mystic countries. I guess I'm included in the last group.

Back in the mouth of San Diego harbor, whatever unspent film remains aboard the *Avanti* is used up on military hardware. If talk is any clue as to what is in a mind, the All-American Boy in the Chicago Bears cap has forgotten he saw a gray whale; the jokes continue where they left off.

In a few hours I'll once again head for an airport, through the eucalyptus, pines, palms, tussock grasses, cane thickets, railway sidings, broken glass, ground-covering vines, faded letters on white stucco, spiky-leafed hedges, and corrugated green fiberglass fences that make up my image of Southern California. And again I'll step onto an airplane, to be taken far into the sky over desert and mountain landscapes and finally deposited almost at my doorstep, all in a single morning.

How will my notes sum up this trip through a land made hallowed by Steinbeck's journal, Rafe's teaching, and Glen's insistence that I go? Maybe those cheers upon seeing a whale, aboard the *Avanti,* are the essence of wonder to be taken home as a souvenir. Yes, I think, if I could shut up some guy in a Bears cap, make him at least keep quiet while his companions cheered for anything nonhuman — beetles, flies, mosquitoes, small fish, tapeworms, crawdads, metamorphic rock, lava flows, not just whales — then I would have come home with what I left to find.

Acknowledgments
Notes
References

Acknowledgments

Raphael Payne supplied an enormous amount of material for this book, including correspondence, interviews, publications from his personal library, maps, and class handouts, much of it information unavailable from public sources. He also read the manuscript, parts of it several times, and offered his comments and criticisms. His wife, Jan, and son, Luke, have shared their home and stories. It is difficult to express adequately my appreciation for this help. If any of you begin such a project, I sincerely hope you find someone like Rafe Payne.

Glen Dappen also contributed significantly to this work. He is a person who leaves no stone unturned, nothing to chance, no reservation unmade, no observation unrecorded. Numerous times, when my own notes were incomplete, I called Glen. He never failed to have everything I had forgotten or not recorded: pictures, addresses, names, the most minute details of a shared experience, everything. He made it possible for me to go to Baja California by making so many of the travel arrangements.

Notes

1. Thoughts over Colorado

The first three pages of this chapter were written on the airplane between Lincoln, Nebraska, and Denver, Colorado, on January 2, 1989. Sources consist mostly of newspaper and magazine stories as well as a wide variety of technical literature, read and partly assimilated over the past thirty years.

2. Mosaics

The James Hutton story is told beautifully in McPhee, *Basin and Range*. Discussions of ventifaction and desert varnish formation can be found in a number of books; I reviewed the material in Brown, *Desert Biology*. In addition, Dr. Sam Treves, professor of geology at the University of Nebraska, looked over my rocks and pictures and provided an extraordinarily insightful and all-too-brief lesson in geology. References on the use of mosaics in Mexican art and architecture are not particularly common in American libraries; the comments in this chapter are based on material from Calvert, *Mexico;* Kirby, *Mexican Landscape Architecture from the Street and from Within;* and Stein, *Mexico.*

3. Cacti

The common names of cacti vary locally. The jumping and teddy-bear chollas are actually the same plant. Mexican names can sound especially romantic to the Anglo ear. Succulents have attracted a dedicated following of both professional and amateur collectors; thus the literature is as varied as their common names. Benson, *Cacti of the United States and Canada,* is an excellent and highly readable source of information for the professional and layperson alike (we may all be laypeople when it comes to cacti!). The wood rat midden story is told with rather mind-boggling elegance in the articles by Van Devender and Van Devender and Spaulding.

4. Mike's Mountain

Mike's Mountain is actually Cerro Santa Ana. It appears on the map by Gastil, Phillips, and Allison as a bright yellow island of volcanic and metamorphic rock in a sea of alluvium. The Campbells' note has been in Mike's shelter for at least four years as of this writing. Don and Susie Campbell talked with me at length about Mike, and the material about his personal life and the building of the trail comes from those interviews.

The references to Cochimi language and culture are from Martinez, *A History of Lower California.* The Anderson quote is from "Geology of Islands and Neighboring Land Areas." Information about the age of islands can be found in Gastil, Minch, and Phillips, "The Geology and Age of the Islands," and about volcanoes in the books by De La Torre and Mooser.

5. Sacred Places

The transformation of Eric Blair is described in Stansky and Abrahams, *Orwell: The Transformation.* My copy was given to me by a woman named Blair Udale. The symbolic animals are described in the papers by Janovy and Kutish and by Janovy, Ferdig, and McDowell. Martinez, *A History of Lower California,* was also useful.

6. On the Beach

This chapter is an almost literal description of a typical biology class field trip. For the casual stroller, any number of shore guides are available, ranging from the highly introductory to the nearly professional. They include Abbott, *American Seashells;* Johnson and Snook, *Seashore Animals of the Pacific Coast;* and Morris, Abbott, and Haderlie, *Intertidal Invertebrates of California.*

7. Keeper of the Keys

There is a relatively large body of literature on the behavior and ecology of hermit crabs, much of it including various species of *Clibanarius* but not necessarily *C. digueti.* The reference sections of virtually all recent works on hermit crabs cite papers by B. A. Hazlett, a pioneer and important contributor to our knowledge of these fascinating animals. The articles by Fotheringham and by Vance are also reasonably accessible and understandable.

8. Rock Pelicans

The biological material in this chapter is derived from personal observations. However, the papers by Schreiber and Van Tets are fairly readable, even for the nonprofessional, and contain some rather amazing information that will be of interest to serious bird watchers on the coasts. The historical background can be found in two wonderful sources: Ley, *Dawn of Zoology,* and Moore, Deyrup-Olsen, and Mayer, "Science as a Way of Knowing."

9. The Gastropod's Gestalt

Most of the shell identifications were made with the aid of the field guides by Abbott and Brusca.

10. El Coyote

This chapter is an almost literal description of the events. The friends who study shark tapeworms and write stories are Janine Caira, a faculty member at the University of Connecticut, and her companion, Evan Jolitz, respectively.

11. To Build a Museum

The comments about the University of Nebraska State Museum are based on my own notes and letters, the legislative records of the state of Nebraska, and stories from both of the Lincoln, Nebraska, newspapers, the *Journal* and the *Star*. Everything about UNSM in this chapter is a matter of public record, some of it front page (newspaper archives for late 1984 and early 1985).

The material on the Museo de Bahía de los Ángeles and its history was obtained from visits, copies of correspondence, museum newsletters, newspaper clippings, and interviews with Wiley Roberson, Fort Worth, Texas; Rafe Payne, Biola University; Lane McDonald, Mira Costa College; José Mercadé, Glendale College; and Carolina Espinoza, Bahía de los Ángeles, the curator of the museum. All these individuals talked at length about the beginnings of the museum and provided their versions of the original stimulus. As you might suspect, these versions differed. Few things are as elusive as ideas; they get spread around a great deal before suddenly taking on a tangible form, and by that time it's usually too late to pin down their birth. Everyone I talked to, however, was clear about the role of Carolina Espinoza; without her there would be no museum.

The Bahía museum, like all museums, is still in need of help. T-shirt sales are the major source of revenue; they are sold at the museum and by Meche and Memo Galvan at Los Licores. Tax-deductible donations can be sent to Natural History and Cultural Museum, Bahía de los Ángeles, c/o Carolina Espinoza, 4459 Maple Avenue, La Mesa, California 92041, or in care of José Mercadé, Glendale Community College–Baja Student Club, 1500 North Verdugo Road, Glendale, California 91208.

The collision of Robert Graham's boat with the gray whale occurred in the summer of 1981; Mr. Graham was kind enough to recount the entire experience over the telephone. The information on fin whales comes mainly from Morzer Bruyns *Field Guide of Whales and Dolphins.*

12. Ordovician Earrings

The major work on the invertebrate fossil record is the many-volume *Treatise on Invertebrate Paleontology,* edited by Moore. Although a number of single-volume texts exist, all refer back to the *Treatise.*

13. Guerrero Negro

There is an extensive literature, both historical and technical, on salt mining and manufacture. The geological library of any major university will provide access to this rather startling body of knowledge. Dr. Phleger, who served as a geological consultant to the salt company, was kind enough to talk to me over the telephone about the operations at Guerrero Negro.

14. Scammon's Lagoon

Whaling has a vast and rich literature: history, fiction, nonfiction, and technical information. Jones, Swartz, and Leatherwood, *The Gray Whale,* is a remarkable work that summarizes an enormous amount of information on the gray whale and gives an extensive bibliography. It is also unusual among technical biology books in being fairly easy to read and understand. The television industry statistics come from the 1990 *World Almanac.*

15. Mechanics

Much of my interest in automobiles as an example of technology comes from time spent with my father-in-law, Glenn Oneth of El Reno, Oklahoma, now deceased. Glenn was a mechanic and service manager in the local Ford garage. Rick Murrane, Rafe's teaching assistant at Biola, supplied the details of his experience with the university van, at least the part I didn't observe directly. Bill Moser, student at the University of Nebraska, actually walked down the arroyo near Ensenada and relayed his impressions of the junk.

The motor industry statistics are from the 1990 *World Almanac* and Hoffman, *Murder on the Highway;* fraudulent repairs are discussed in Norris, *Auto Repair Frauds;* psychological studies on high-risk drivers are given in Weiers, *Licensed to Kill,* which has a bibliography.

16. Life Long Dreams

Glen Dappen made sure, as best he could, that all of his students would actually see a whale. He thus arranged housing in San Diego and made the *Avanti* reservations. The narrative in this chapter is derived from two excursions a year apart; although all of it is true, the two years' events are mixed.

References

Abbott, R. T. *American Seashells,* 2nd ed. New York: Van Nostrand Reinhold, 1974.

Anderson, C. A. "Geology of Islands and Neighboring Land Areas." Part I. In *1940 E. W. Scripps Cruise to the Gulf of California.* Geological Society of America Memoirs, no. 43 (1950): i–vii, 1–53.

Aschmann, H. *The Central Desert of Baja California: Demography and Ecology.* Berkeley: University of California Press, 1959.

Benson, L. *The Cacti of the United States and Canada.* Stanford: Stanford University Press, 1982.

Brown, G. W., ed. *Desert Biology,* vols. 1 and 2. New York: Academic Press, 1968, 1974.

Brusca, R. C. *Common Intertidal Invertebrates of the Gulf of California.* Tucson: University of Arizona Press, 1980.

Buxbaum, F. *Morphology of Cacti.* Pasadena: Abbey Garden Press, 1950.

Calvert, P. *Mexico.* New York: Praeger, 1973.

Curtis, Edward S. *The North American Indian,* vol. 11. Norwood, Mass.: Plimpton Press, 1916.

De La Torre, E. Y. *Volcanes de Mexico.* Mexico City: Aguilar, 1971.

Dewees, C. M. *Gyotaku — Japanese Fish Printing.* Leaflet no. 2548.

Davis: University of California, Division of Agricultural Sciences, 1978.

Dietrich, R. V. *Stones*. San Francisco: W. H. Freeman, 1980.

Durham, J. W. "Megascopic Paleontology and Marine Stratigraphy." Part II. In *1940* E. W. Scripps *Cruise to the Gulf of California*. Geological Society of America Memoirs, no. 43 (1950): i–viii, 1–216.

Dyson, F. *Disturbing the Universe*. New York: Harper and Row, 1979.

———. *Infinite in All Directions*. New York: Harper and Row, 1988.

Fotheringham, N. "Population Consequence of Shell Utilization by Hermit Crabs." *Ecology* 57 (1976): 570–87.

———. "Hermit Crab Shells as a Limiting Resource (Decapoda, Paguridae)." *Crustaceana* 31 (1976): 193–99.

Fussel, P. 1989. "The Real War 1939–1945." *The Atlantic* 264 (1989): 32–40.

Gastil, G., J. Minch, and R. Phillips. "The Geology and Age of the Islands." In *Island Biogeography in the Sea of Cortez*, ed. T. J. Case and M. L. Cody. Berkeley: University of California Press, 1983.

Gastil, R. G., R. P. Phillips, and E. C. Allison. *Reconnaissance Geological Map of the State of Baja California*. Geological Society of America, 1971.

Gerhard. P., and H. E. Gulick. *Lower California Guidebook*. Glendale, Calif.: Arthur H. Clark, 1964.

Gould. S. J. *Wonderful Life*. New York: W. W. Norton, 1989.

Hausback, B. P. "Cenozoic Volcanic and Tectonic Evolution of Baja California Sur, Mexico." In *Geology of the Baja California Peninsula*, ed. V. A. Frizzell. Los Angeles: Society of Economic Paleontologists and Mineralogists, Pacific Section, 1984.

Hazlett, B. A. "The Behavioral Ecology of Hermit Crabs." *Annual Review of Ecology and Systematics* 12 (1981): 1–22.

Hoffman, M. S., ed. *World Almanac and Book of Facts*. New York: Scripps Howard, 1990.

Hoffman, R. N. *Murder on the Highway*. New York: A. S. Barnes, 1966.

Hofstadter, D. R. *Metamagical Themas*. New York: Basic Books, 1985.

Janovy, J., Jr., and G. W. Kutish. "A Model of Encounters Between Host and Parasite Populations." *Journal of Theoretical Biology* 134 (1988): 391–401.

Janovy, J., Jr., M. T. Ferdig, and M. A. McDowell. "A Model of Dynamic Behavior of a Parasite Species Assemblage." *Journal of Theoretical Biology* 142 (1988): 517–29.

Johnson, M. E., and H. J. Snook. *Seashore Animals of the Pacific Coast.* New York: Macmillan, 1927; reprint, Dover, 1967.

Jones, M. L., S. L. Swartz, and S. Leatherwood, eds. *The Gray Whale* Eschrichtius robustus. New York: Academic Press, 1984.

Kirby, R. G. *Mexican Landscape Architecture from the Street and from Within.* Tucson: University of Arizona Press, 1972.

Kostick, D. S. "Salt." In *Minerals Yearbook,* vol. 1. Washington, D.C.: U.S. Department of the Interior, 1986.

Krutch, J. W. *The Forgotten Peninsula.* New York: William Morrow, 1961.

Ley, W. *Dawn of Zoology.* Englewood Cliffs, N.J.: Prentice-Hall, 1968.

Mailer, N. *Cannibals and Christians.* New York: Dial Press, 1966.

Martinez, P. L. (trans. Ethel Duffy Turner). *A History of Lower California.* Mexico: Editorial Baja California, 1960.

McPhee, J. *Basin and Range.* New York: Farrar, Straus, and Giroux, 1981.

Moore, J. A., I. Deyrup-Olsen, and W. V. Mayer. "Science as a Way of Knowing: V-Form and Function." *American Zoologist* 28: (1988): 441–808.

Moore, R. C., ed. *Treatise on Invertebrate Paleontology.* Part N, vol. 1: *Mollusca 6, Bivalvia.* Lawrence, Kans.: Geological Society of America, and University of Kansas, 1969.

Mooser, F., H. Meyer-Abich, and A. R. McBirney. *Catalogue of the Active Volcanoes and Solfatara Fields of Central America,* part 6. Naples: International Volcanological Association, 1958.

Morris, R. H., D. P. Abbott, and E. C. Haderlie. *Intertidal Invertebrates of California.* Stanford: Stanford University Press, 1980.

Morzer Bruyns, W. F. J. *Field Guide of Whales and Dolphins.* Amsterdam: N. V. Uitgeverij, 1971.

Nickerson, R. *The Friendly Whales.* San Francisco: Chronicle Books, 1987.

Norris, M. 1976. *Auto Repair Frauds: How to Prevent Your Car from*

Driving You into the Poorhouse. New York: Arco, 1976.

Phleger, F. B. "Sedimentology of Guerrero Negro Lagoon, Baja California, Mexico." In *Submarine Geology and Geophysics,* ed. W. F. Whittard and R. Bradshaw. London: Butterworth, 1965.

———. "A Modern Evaporite Deposit in Mexico." *American Society of Petroleum Geologists Bulletin* 53 (1969): 824–29.

Phleger, F. B., and G. C. Ewing. "Sedimentology and Oceanography of Coastal Lagoons in Baja California, Mexico." *Geological Society of America Bulletin* 73 (1962): 145–82.

Roberts, N. C. *Baja California Plant Field Guide.* La Jolla, Calif.: Natural History Publishing Company, 1989.

Rocamora, J., and J. M. Rafols. "Salt Plants at Torrevieja [Spain] and Their Operation." In *Second Symposium on Salt.* Cleveland: Northern Ohio Geological Society, 1966.

Scammon, C. M. *The Marine Mammals of the Northwestern Coast of North America.* New York: G. P. Putnam's Sons, 1874; facsimile ed., Dover, 1968.

Schreiber, R. W. *Maintenance Behavior and Communication in the Brown Pelican.* Ornithological Monographs no. 22. American Ornithologists' Union, 1977.

Sheehan, N. *A Bright Shining Lie.* New York: Random House, 1988.

Stansky, P., and W. Abrahams. *Orwell: The Transformation.* London: Constable, 1979.

Stein, R. C. *Mexico.* Chicago: Children's Press, 1984.

Steinbeck, J., and E. F. Ricketts. *Sea of Cortez: A Leisurely Journey of Travel and Research, with a Scientific Appendix Comprising Materials for a Source Book on the Marine Animals of the Panamic Faunal Province.* New York: Viking, 1941.

Vance, R. R. "Competition and Mechanisms of Coexistence in Three Sympatric Species of Intertidal Hermit Crabs." *Ecology* 53 (1972): 1062–74.

———. "The Role of Shell Adequacy in Behavioral Interactions Involving Hermit Crabs." *Ecology* 53 (1972): 1075–83.

Van Devender, T. R. 1977. "Holocene Woodlands in the Southwestern Deserts." *Science* 198(1977): 189–93.

Van Devender, T. R., and W. G. Spaulding. "Development of Vegetation and Climate in the Southwestern United States." *Science* 204 (1979): 701–10.

Van Tets, G. F. *A Comparative Study of Some Social Communication Patterns in the Pelecaniformes.* Ornithological Monographs no. 2. American Ornithologists' Union, 1965.

Weiers, R. M. *Licensed to Kill.* New York: Chilton, 1968.

Zwinger, A. *A Desert Country near the Sea.* New York: Harper and Row, 1983.

———. *The Mysterious Lands.* New York: E. P. Dutton, 1989.